THE unHOLY LAND

THE unHOLY LAND

A.C. FORREST

McClelland and Stewart Limited
Toronto

The Canadian Publishers
McClelland and Stewart Limited
25 Hollinger Road, Toronto 374

Printed in Canada

Fifth printing and first paperback edition, 1972

Clothbound 0–7710–3163–7
Paperback 0–7710–3161–0

Acknowledgements

Israel, Miracle in the Desert, Terence Prittie, Penguin Books.
Israel and the Arabs, Maxime Rodinson, Penguin Special.
The Arabs in Israel, A Digest of Sabri Jiryis's book, published
       by the Fifth of June Society.
Soldiering for Peace, Major-General Carl von Horn, David
       McKay Company, Inc.
Between Arab and Israeli, Lieutenant-General E.L.M. Burns,
       The Institute for Palestine Studies,
       Clarke, Irwin and Company Ltd.
Jewish Labor Bund, 1897-1957, International Jewish Labor
       Bund.
The Evasive Peace, John H. Davis, John Murray.

Contents

Introduction

It seems that every Middle East fact-finding group – of which there have been many recently – emphasizes the need for greater understanding of the complex Arab-Israeli issues. This book is my contribution to such understanding. It is a summary of what I have seen and heard in the Middle East and what I have learned about the struggle since June 1967.

Although I had been to the Middle East several times before, I returned in July 1967 to report on the refugee situation for a syndicate of North American church magazines. I went back again for ten months between September 1968 and June 1969 and again for the month of May 1970. During these years I have come to share with other outsiders who know and appreciate the Arab and Israeli people, a three-fold concern: that positive steps be taken to avoid another war that may engulf us all; that the long suffering of the Palestine refugees be ended; and that the security of the Jewish people be assured.

It is only after clearing away the smothering accumulation of propaganda and distortion which always confounds an intelligent discussion of Arab-Israeli relations, and letting the facts get through, that we who live outside may evaluate the issues and support – or even initiate – policies that may end the strife.

During my ten months stint, when I was editor-at-large of The *United Church Observer*, writing for *Presbyterian Life*, The *United Church Herald* (us), *Together* (Methodist), The *Episcopalian*, The *Lutheran* and a few others, my family and

I lived in Beirut. I travelled regularly to Jordan, Syria, and the UAR, and on four occasions to Israel. Usually I crossed the Jordan River at the Allenby Bridge.

There were no difficulties at any time with either Arabs or Israelis, although a Kuwaiti official demanded to see my "other" passport once and when he saw an Israeli stamp on it refused a visa, though he was very nice about it. A telephone call or two worked that out. It is necessary when securing visas or other permits to do things the way the Israeli and Arab officials want them done and not be upset when the bureaucrats waste a little time on the paper work. After all, despite the cease-fire arrangements, there is a war on in the Middle East and the stakes are high. The Israelis are security-conscious and the Arabs tend to be suspicious of strangers. But I had no real unpleasantness and I speak with considerable enthusiasm of both Israeli and Arab hospitality. They are such nice people that I wish they could all enjoy permanent peace and prosperity.

It was my privilege during my many visits to have interviews with a number of leaders and officials in both Israel and the Arab world. I think, however, I learned more from my many contacts with UN and Red Cross officials and representatives of other agencies. I admit with some embarrassment though that while I visited the area three times, talked with many people, and did quite a bit of reading, I didn't really come to understand what the struggle was all about until after the June war.

When I was forced that summer to do my homework and discovered how different the true story was from what I had heard and read in the West, I felt betrayed by the newspapers and broadcast media I had trusted. I still feel betrayed when I read the editorials, letters to the editor, and some of the news despatches in my daily newspapers, or listen to a fundamentalist preacher explain, after he has had a free guided tour to Israel, how it was God's will for Israel to take Palestine.

There are many things this book does not attempt to do. I do not, for example, try to tell again what has been so adequately and frequently told on television and in the press, the story of Israeli accomplishments on the land where the Jewish people have been building a Jewish state. I cannot help but believe that through all their sufferings and persecution, so often at the hands of people called Christians, the Jews have emerged a superior race. (Of course, that does suggest others are inferior.) In art, music, drama – in the making of books, and the miracles on the land, in so many things, Israel has excelled. True, the US and world Jewry have poured in billions to do it with, but many peoples would have squandered much of such aid. None, I suspect – although the Japanese and Germans might have given it a real try – would have accomplished so much, so quickly, as Israel has.

Nor have I dealt with the military accomplishments of Israel, which are superb, or the military failures of the Arabs, which are profound. I have also failed to report much of what is happening in the Arab world. I do not describe its one-time greatness or the promise of its emergence again. It is true that there is a lot this book doesn't attempt to do.

However, I have tried to tell what has led to the present conflict that threatens us all; I report what the situation is, especially among the Palestine refugees. I have been very critical of Israel, for I believe that Israel carries great responsibility for the present situation; and it is Israel which could, with honour, take the initial steps that would lead to peace. The Arabs cannot in honour do very much as long as Israel occupies their lands and evicts and suppresses their people.

For expressing my opinions and publishing my conclusions I have been called an anti-Semite and other things. This used to hurt very much, until I learned what distinguished company I was in. Even Arnold Toynbee! When critics of Israeli policy or Zionist philosophy, and in some instances even those who without attaching blame told the story of the Palestine refugees, were first called anti-Semitic, they were discredited and in some cases professionally destroyed. Now, it hurts about as much to be called an anti-Semite by a Zionist as it does to be called a Communist by a John Bircher. This is too bad, for anti-Semitism is a nasty thing and the sting should not be taken from it. It is demeaning to treat any person as something lesser or inferior because of his race, religion, or name. It demeans the object and the subject. However, the label has been pinned

viii

on so many so often by such fanatical and foolish men that it isn't taken seriously any more.

As a matter of fact, when I first became interested in this subject I suppose I was mildly anti-Arab. Certainly, like almost everyone else, I was pro-Israeli. When I remember what I was taught in school about the Crusades and some of the stories I have read about "dirty Arabs" and "wily Arabs" and "thieving Arabs," I realize how badly we were prepared for what has happened. We have been sensitized to the nasty expressions of anti-Semitism to which we used to be exposed. We know something about Martin Luther and other persecutors of Jews. We even are told that the New Testament is anti-Semitic. But most of us know Jews, have Jewish friends and profound admiration for many Jewish people, and we have been appalled by our inheritance of Christian guilt. But we didn't know Arabs, or their history or their culture.

In my original anti-Arabism I suppose I was rather typical of reasonably intelligent, fairly well-informed, well-intentioned church-going, newspaper-reading Westerners. I had my pro-Israeli, anti-Arab leanings. To me the Jews were God's chosen people, Jerusalem was His Holy City, and Palestine His Holy Land. It was a sign of God's special favour that when General Allenby entered Jerusalem the Turks surrendered without a shot. It seemed good that after long centuries of wandering the Jews could go back to the land of their fathers, and not unreasonable that the people who had lived there – Arabs who went around on donkeys and camels and neglected their land – would have to move over and let them in. I had inherited some of these notions from my Church and Sunday School. To me the Holy Land was so romantic that I was even rather startled when I first heard an outboard motor on the Sea of Galilee and somewhat offended when I saw young people skiing on its sacred waters. I was even shocked by seeing a prison in Israel – and by learning that many Israeli Jews did not believe in God.

Well, that's not the way I found it. This story of mine may be condemned by extremists from both sides. I throw out this challenge, though, which I have made many times without anyone yet taking me up: Check with those who know the story, that is, anyone who has lived or worked for some reasonable length of time on both sides, anyone from the UN or its agencies, or any of the scores of "foreigners" at work in the Middle East. They may disagree on some details. I will be surprised if they disagree on any essential point of my conclusions.

They are that:

In attempting to solve the Jewish problem by recommending the partition of Palestine the world inflicted a grave injustice on the Palestinian Arabs. There is little hope of lasting peace in the Middle East until there is redress of that injustice.

The Palestinian refugees are not just the innocent victims of war who fled their homes in Palestine in panic and must not be allowed back because they would threaten the security of Israel: many of them were ruthlessly driven out as part of an Israeli master-plan to rid Palestine of its citizens in order to build a "Jewish" state.

The Palestinians are not just being kept as "political pawns" by the Arab states, but are determined to resist settlement and assimilation and return to their homes in Palestine.

The Arabs who remained in Israel have been exploited and repressed by the Israeli Jews. Most Arabs in Occupied Territory are bitterly hostile to the Occupation and loyal to the fedayeen. Israel consistently violates the Fourth Geneva Convention in her treatment of civilians and flouts the unanimous decisions of the United Nations General Assembly and Security Council. Israel is now a racist and aggressive state.

These are the conclusions which, I submit, any objective student of the Middle East will reach if he reads the UN documents, visits the area for some reasonable length of time, talks to the experts, and meets the people. He will find many other things I have omitted. But these, it seems to me, are facts which must be known and understood if we are to have peace and justice in the Holy Land.

Foreword to the 1972 Edition

Shortly after this book was first published in Canada, in January 1971, I received a letter from a lawyer in Baltimore, seeking more information about the refugee lad I had met in Gaza (see page 3). He said he would like to provide further education for the boy in an American school, if it could be arranged.

It has been arranged.

A number of readers, disturbed by the ongoing tragedy of the Palestinian people, were moved to similar generous acts. While private charity is not the answer to the Middle East problem it is needed, and it helps, and I am grateful that this book has contributed.

Of course the reactions to *The Unholy Land* were not all such pleasant ones. Within days of publication I began to learn something more of what happens to critics of Israeli policies and Zionist philosophy. For the book to be denounced was no surprise. That it should create a "public furor", as prophesied by Peter Worthington of the *Toronto Telegram* or stir up an "unholy row", as predicted by the *Calgary Herald,* was rather startling.

It was assumed it might be denied some of the usual outlets, both stores and libraries, and that reviews by some friendly critics would be suppressed by unfriendly editors and publishers. The assumption was correct.

However, reviews and letters to the editor were numerous, good, bad, and vitriolic. They were fewer and harsher in the big cities with their large Jewish populations.

At the *Toronto Telegram*, a large and zealously pro-Zionist daily that has since died, the book editor told me that he approached five reviewers who turned down the assignment because they did not want "to get involved". But Douglas Fisher wrote two columns and Peter Worthington of the *Telegram* wrote a feature. Fisher had recently returned from both sides in the Middle East. "I agree with his presentation of the Palestinian refugee problem. It fits what I saw and heard and read about but I shiver for Dr. Forrest", he wrote.

I did shiver when the book was withdrawn from sale by Coles book stores, the largest chain in Canada. But my recovery was immediate when the story of the "ban" became national. One group picketed one of the Coles stores, and their protest was televised. After three days of "no comment", the head of Coles issued a statement saying, *"The Unholy Land* was a complete non-seller". His timing was beautiful – for me. For that day it made the *Toronto Star's* syndicated "National Best Seller List". It continued there for three months, while the first three printings were sold out.

Mr. Sol Littman, a public relations expert imported from the US to help the Canada-Israel Committee, collected data from bookstores designed to prove that any success the book might have was not because of merit or interest but because of the controversy. It was implied that the controversy had been a promotion gimmick dreamed up by the publisher and/or the author. Mr. Littman circulated his findings to the media and the debate was on again. The publisher dismissed the suggestions as "ludicrous", and ordered another printing. Pro-Israeli women writers in Montreal and Winnipeg took up the hue and cried into their columns. Mrs. Marion Lepkin was reminded, she told the readers of the *Winnipeg Free Press*, "of the ritual drinking of the blood of Christian babies. . . ." In Montreal, Mrs. Betty Shapiro found *The Unholy Land* to be "a pro-Arab, anti-Israeli broadside". Sales in Montreal and Winnipeg went up. "Do you know who is buying it here?" a Winnipeg book salesman asked me. I answered correctly, "Your Jewish customers."

Almost every day I was reminded that there are great numbers of well-informed, non-Zionist Jewish people who are embarrassed by Zionists who presume to speak for them. They don't take seriously the suggestion that those who may criticize the policies of Israel are prejudiced against Jewish people.

I suppose every writer of a book dreams sometimes of becoming a "best-seller". I did not have such ambitions for my modest and very personal report. But then I didn't know that the Canadian Zionists would be, for me, like a ban in Boston. The fourth printing was sold out in eight months and within the year it was decided to publish in paperback.

Although these and other funny things happened on the way to the present (fifth) printing, one's skin needed to be much tougher than mine to remain unscathed by the charges of bigotry, bias, and anti-this and that. However, I have found unanimous support from those who have been to both sides of the Middle East, especially from UN, Church, and academic people. There have been humbling expressions of gratitude from North American Arabs, who may not agree with my proposals for settlement, but who appreciate any attempt to understand.

Best of all, I have been reassured by Jewish supporters, some of them booksellers, many of them young, and a few who have lived in Israel. They brave the vilification of zealots in their own community to promote the cause of understanding, truth, and justice. They know the truth of James Reston's comment in the *New York Times*, "You can put it down as a general rule that any criticism of Israel's policies will be attacked as anti-Semitism."

We, the publisher and I, had hoped when *The Unholy Land* was being readied for publication that it would appear simultaneously in Canada, the USA, and possibly Britain. But American publishers have become wary of this kind of book. One told me: "I like it. I would like to publish it. But frankly I am afraid."

However, Devin-Adair, a house which has successfully marketed such books as Alfred Lilienthal's *The Other Side of the Coin* and *There Goes the Middle East*, has published this edition, and it has also been translated into Arabic and published by An Nahar in Beirut.

Recent developments in the Middle East have been summarized in a postscript beginning on page 173.

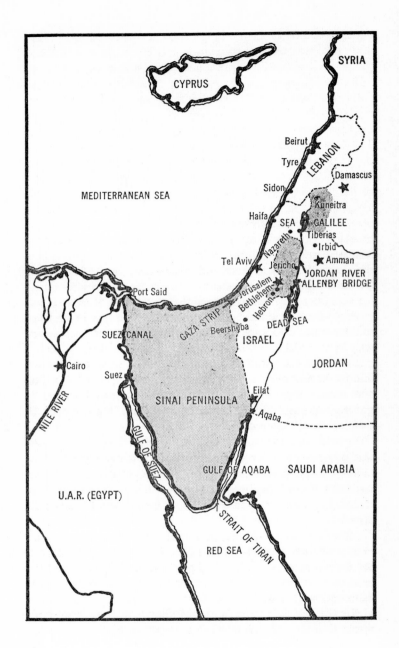

one

The Holy Land – 1970

ON MAY 12TH, 1970, I CROSSED THE ALLENBY BRIDGE FROM East Jordan to Israeli-occupied Palestine. An Arab family was huddled in the shade of the willows on the West shore under the watchful eye of a well-armed Israeli guard. Few were crossing that day and none seemed to give more than a quick glance at the refugees. In a world of over two million homeless, another man, wife, and four small children stirred little interest.

Later, after I – with my Canadian passport – was given a smiling welcome by Israeli officials, I waited to share a taxi with others who might be going to Jerusalem. I saw that woman and her children again, being loaded into the back of a police van. The mother lugged a big and battered old suitcase, held together with rope. A blonde, sunburned Israeli officer lifted the suitcase into the van and drove away.

My taxi-driver explained. The woman, with her children, had been brought by the police to meet her husband at the bridge. He was a refugee on the East Bank; she and the children were refugees in Gaza. They had been separated since the June war in 1967. The man had never seen his youngest child until that morning; two of the other three children did not recognize him. She had hoped, the driver explained, to cross over to East Jordan; and the Israelis had provided transport, as their policy is, to the bridge. But the Jordanians wouldn't have her. The husband asked to return with his family to Gaza. The Israelis refused that.

"They have their reasons," an Arab explained. "The Jordanians have already let forty thousand Gaza refugees cross over, and the Jordan camps are overflowing. So they have stopped it." It had appeared that Israel was conniving to get as many Palestinians out of Gaza and off their hands as possible.

"As for the Israelis," the Arab went on, "her husband may have been a member of the Palestine army, or perhaps he belongs to Fateh."

So the mother and children went back to refugee camp life in Gaza. And the father returned to Jordan, alone. Later, when I told Mr. Shukri Saleh of the Near East Council of Churches about the incident, he said, "Yes, it is very sad. But there are thousands like them."

A few hours later I was taken from Jerusalem to the old Kalendia refugee camp north of the Holy City. That afternoon the Israeli police had moved in, set up loud speakers, ordered the people – there were over three thousand refugees in Kalendia – into their houses, and told them to open their windows. The Israelis went directly to a seven-room house between the mosque and the school basketball courts, gave the people ten minutes to get out, laid nine sticks of dynamite, and blew the house to bits. Fifty rabbits, some turkeys, and most household goods were beneath the rubble. An expensive-looking incubator for turkey eggs lay broken besides the ruins. "He got the incubator out but the Israelis smashed it," a bystander said. A teen-aged girl was weeping. She had worked and saved and purchased a sewing machine. It went under too.

"We try to get them to bulldoze these houses," Alan Graham of UNRWA said. "That way they don't damage the other buildings. But this is a nice neat job. They've had a lot of practice."

The owner of the house had been taken to hospital in a state of shock. Camp children were moving about quietly as though they were at a funeral. Some women were squatting and weeping among household utensils they had saved. Men were standing about talking angrily.

I asked them what the man had done. "We don't know, but the police arrested one of his sons a month ago and took

2

him away." It was presumed the son had been made to talk. Sometimes houses are blown up because the owners have not reported on subversive activities of their neighbours.

I said it was very sad.

"There are over seven thousand cases like it," I was told.

The Israeli officials admit they have blown up about seven hundred Arab homes but the Arabs count all the houses that have been destroyed when an entire village has been demolished, and those destroyed when as many as eighty houses have been levelled as a collective reprisal. The Israelis apparently count only "individual" dynamitings.

I went from Kalendia to Gaza, roundabout by the Latrun Valley where the villages of Beit Nuba, Yalu, and Emmaus used to be. They are all gone – demolished after the June war. Arabs have not been permitted back.

In Gaza the streets were almost empty and half the shops were closed. The last time I had been there, in August 1967, the streets were jammed and the stores were doing a flourishing business with Israeli bargain-hunters. There are a lot of demolished houses in Gaza and the population is sullen.

"Where are the people?" I asked my escort, Mr. Ad Van Goor of the Near East Council of Churches.

"They are sitting at home – afraid," he said.

In an orange grove operated by the NECC for a charitable fund, a handsome eighteen-year old boy served us big juicy oranges and brought a vessel of water and a towel so we could wipe our hands. He was blonde and blue-eyed, built like the captain of our high school football team back home. He was a gentle and courteous lad who spoke quietly in Arabic to Mr. Van Goor.

"He's worried about his future," Mr. Van Goor said. "He is through school and has completed an UNRWA vocational course but there is no work. There is, for him, no future. But it is better for him to be here with his father than in the camp."

I kept asking about it – worrying Mr. Van Goor.

"Look," he said, "you can't let it get to you. There are thousands like him."

The people of Gaza were troubled because a number of their

3

most prominent citizens had been banished to the desert. "Oh, they are fed and watered, but they are all alone. And they have not been charged, or tried, or sentenced, and they don't know when they will get back."

"To spend a few months alone on the desert destroys a man," a Red Cross representative told me.

Of all the depressing areas in the Middle East, Gaza is the worst. The conquered Arabs live in an atmosphere heavy with hatred. The terrorists are everywhere. Van Goor switched his Jerusalem car for one with local license plates as soon as we arrived, for the suspicious Jerusalem plates might be the target of a grenade.

Yet in the almost daily incidents the Gazan Arabs are constant losers. The Israeli military's casualty count from incidents since June 1967 is "ninety Gazans killed, four hundred wounded; three Israeli soldiers killed, twenty-six wounded, and fourteen Israeli civilians wounded."

As I went north from Gaza the American-made Skyhawks were darting about the sky. The highway was heavy with army trucks and young hitchhiking Israeli soldiers. "They are training night and day," my driver said.

In Tel Aviv it was hectic and crowded. I found troubled Israelis who said out loud that what Israel was doing to the Arabs was stupid and wrong – "this blowing up of houses, this annexation of territory, is wrong. We should have let the refugees back in 1967." Some were intensely loyal to the government's methods; others were bitterly critical.

I went on by bus to Nazareth Most of the passengers were Arabs in working clothes; a few were Jewish. When, a little uncertain, I prepared to get off the bus in downtown Nazareth, the well-dressed Jewish occupants insisted I was making a mistake. They apparently thought I was Jewish and should go on to the new suburb on the hill beyond. I made it off at the next stop – at Mary's well – and took a taxi back to an Arab hotel. It had been forsaken by the Christian tourists and was almost empty.

4

The next day I went with Donald Scott, of Lutheran World Service, to an Israeli kibbutz on the Sea of Galilee to make arrangements to go fishing that night. "We don't fish at night any more," a lady at the desk told me. I asked why. "For thousands of years they fished at night," I said.

"That's what we told our young people when they wanted to try fishing in the daytime," she smiled. "And they said, 'Well, can't we at least try?' So they did, and they caught fish, and now we do most of our fishing in the daytime." Early the next morning Scott and I went out with four Israeli fishermen in a power boat. They went first towards Tiberias, rather aimlessly it seemed to me, then back north to Capernaum. I wondered why they took so long to lower the nets. Then I discovered they had sonar equipment and were waiting till they found a school of fish below. Suddenly an alarm was sounded and the nets were let out quickly. The boat circled and the winches hauled in about two hundred pounds of sardines. The men went to work packing the fish with ice. A few minutes later we caught about four hundred pounds off Gadara.

"The Arabs used to shoot at you here, didn't they?" I asked one of the men. He grinned. "They don't anymore." For twenty years Galilee was on the Syrian border. The Israelis constantly intruded into Syrian territory and the Syrians shelled them from the Golan Heights above.

The shores of Galilee are almost completely occupied by Jewish people. The original Arab residents were driven out in 1947 and 1948, many of them to live on the Golan heights above until 1967, when they were driven eastward again and are now two-time losers near Damascus.

In the afternoon we visited the kindergarten in the kibbutz where the little boys were playing war games in a big sandbox and had made a fine collection of fighting planes from plasticine. "I hope," the teacher told us, "our children won't have to fight when they grow up."

Arab friends in Jerusalem and Bethlehem who knew me from other times told me of sons and daughters away at university in Beirut or Canada or the USA. "No," they hadn't seen

5

them for several years. "No," they didn't expect them to come back. "What is there for them here?" And, in some cases, "They are not allowed to return."

Jews can come from anywhere in the world and instantly be citizens in Israel; Arabs, whose ancestors lived in Palestine for thousands of years, are not permitted to return to their own homes if they were away at university in Amman or Beirut on June 5th, 1967.

Actually, Israel does permit some students to visit their families in Israeli-occupied territory. One undergraduate told me, "I am not going to ask for permission from the Israelis to visit my own land, where my family has lived for centuries." An Armenian teacher in Jerusalem told me, "I have three children in university in Canada and another studying medicine in Beirut. My wife and I are all alone now. I don't want them to come back to this."

After a week I re-crossed the Jordan. Many fruit trees have died in the once irrigated orchards between Jericho and the Jordan through lack of attention since the 1967 war. But the flowers about the empty homes and the empty camps where one hundred thousand Palestinians used to live bloomed as I had never seen them bloom before.

An old lady in our car, who had been given permission to go to Amman to see her son, was unwell. He had been refused admission to Jerusalem to visit her in hospital, so she was going to see him. He met us on the East side of the bridge and carried his mother to his car; he was, I learned, the expelled mayor of Ramallah.

I drove, subdued, past the ruins of what had once been the prosperous little East Bank town of Karameh, built by refugees out of the desert but destroyed by Israeli shells and tanks in 1968. No one lives there now, but a few peasants slip back in the daytime to tend their fields.

So it went for four weeks, as I took my two passports (one for use in the Arab countries and another for Israel) and my American travellers' cheques and journeyed through Lebanon,

Syria, Jordan, Occupied Jordan, and Israel – with a quick trip to Cairo.

I saw Jordan tottering on the verge of civil war. Those who had worked for years to ease suffering among the homeless were half afraid to carry on. The refugees, who had been told by the United Nations for over twenty years that they should be allowed to return or be compensated for lost homes, were militant and bitter. "We can't take you about," my UN friends said. "You had better go with Fateh." So I went with Fateh.

In Egypt I found the west bank of the Suez had been pounded to a shambles and the people who lived there, over half a million of them, scattered about the country. "We had to get Russian anti-aircraft missiles because the Israeli planes come as far as Cairo now," I was told.

In Damascus the streets were filled with soldiers, refugees, and the fedayeen in camouflage. Only four hundred of the one hundred and thirty thousand refugees who fled the Golan Heights and the Kuneitra area in 1967 have been permitted by the Israelis to return home and the resentment towards Israel has deepened.

In Southern Lebanon, on May 28th, I sat in a Fateh mountain hide-out near the frontier and watched the Israelis shelling Hebbariye. About fifteen thousand new Lebanese refugees from the south were heading north. Back in Beirut, where headlines predicted an Israeli invasion, the night clubs were filled, the streets were crowded, and the great Liban Casino was sold out night after night.

I was back in what some still call the Holy Land.

East of the Jordan

ONE MORNING IN EARLY JULY 1967, ROBERT CADIGAN, EDITOR of *Presbyterian Life* in Philadelphia, called me at the Toronto office of the *United Church Observer*. He wanted me to go, he announced, to the Middle East almost immediately, to check on the new refugee problem and report for Interchurch Features.

I demurred. I was busy, and I understood that the so-called new refugee problem was being solved by the UN and the Israeli government.

Over two hundred thousand, we had been told, had fled during the June war. The UN, which ordered the cease-fire, had also said that all those who had left their homes should be allowed to return. This had been echoed by spokesmen for the WCC and some of the larger churches. Israel had said officially through the Knesset that refugees could come back from the East Bank to their empty homes and camps.

"That's not what we are hearing," Bob told me. "There seems to be considerable confusion about the facts. Some of the people may not get back at all. They need tents, food, blankets, medicines." He explained that there was rumoured to be a bad situation in Syria – and Americans and British weren't allowed into Syria – a serious situation in the UAR, and it might be necessary for me to go to Iraq too.

Cadigan also implied that American churchmen who were familiar with the Middle East were convinced that North Americans – and the Europeans to a lesser extent – weren't getting the facts from the newspapers and other media. Some

8

felt the church press had a responsibility to correct the imbalance. The *Christian Science Monitor*, it was said, was the only newspaper on the continent giving balanced information of the Arab-Israeli struggle.

He made another point. It would be easier for a Canadian to travel in the Middle East than for an American.

I went to Ottawa to be briefed by External Affairs people and, as expected, found the MP's and the politicians uninformed and the civil servants well-informed. There were indications that Israel was digging in on the new territories as though she intended to defy the UN, flout international law, and turn the conquered territory into part of a newly enlarged Israel. There were also signs that she might be planning to keep out those who had fled, while informing the world they could return.

I headed for the Holy Land. First I was briefed in New York, then in Geneva, then again in Beirut. Then I went to Amman, the capital of Jordan, and discovered that none of those who had briefed me really knew what was happening on the cease-fire lines.

Mr. Shukri Saleh, a Palestinian and Secretary of the Jordan office of the Near East Council of Churches refugee division, met me and took me to the Philadelphia Hotel. A middle-aged doctor and his wife, refugees from Ramallah, were staying at the Philadelphia. They were refugees for the third time in their lives. Originally they had escaped from Russia and settled in Jaffa. In 1948 they left everything behind and started over in Ramallah. On June 5th they were in Amman when the war broke out.

Mr. Saleh had an eighty-year old friend from Bethlehem with him too. He had been at the Amman airport on June 5th and couldn't get back. His wife was in Bethlehem.

While there, a younger man who said he had "a wife and five kids on the other side," came to tell Shukri he had failed again. For six weeks he had been going every day to the Red Cross, and sometimes up to the Allenby Bridge or what was left of it, trying to get home to his family. He had been in Amman June 5th with his employer's car and wasn't allowed to return.

He said that day he had tried a different way and had gone

with some other refugees to the river and waded over. They made their way through uninhabited parts as far as Jericho and there he was picked up by the Israel police as he was climbing into an Arab taxi. They took him to the bridge and ordered him to sign a paper saying he was leaving the West Bank at his own request. This could have been used later to keep him out for good; he refused. So they took him and some others in a truck to a wild uninhabited part of the Jordan River Bank and ordered them to get out.

"I was sure we were going to be shot, as many have been. I remember thinking it was near the site of Jesus' baptism." They were ordered to wade to the Jordan side. "Tell Hussein that next time we'll come and take Amman too," one of the soldiers shouted at them.

I had had no idea it was this way in Jordan.

"But I understood Israel was letting the people back," I insisted.

"You must have seen that television show too," Mr. Saleh said.

"They let a hundred and forty go back to the West bank for television purposes," someone said. "They filmed them all and we heard it was shown all over the USA. But about six hundred came this way the same day and they didn't take any of their pictures."

"Up in Syria," I was told, "there are ten thousand from the Golan Heights living in the fields without any shelter, and Israel is still driving them out of the territory she occupied. We don't know what is happening in Egypt."

If this were true then I had been betrayed by the press and media I had trusted. If it were true that Israel really did intend to keep the territories she had acquired by force and intended to obstruct the return of the new refugees, then peace would be quite impossible in the Middle East.

It would mean that Israel was telling the UN to go fly a kite, that she was thumbing her nose at the rest of the world, that she was paying no attention to the voices of great Jewish thinkers who urged reconciliation. It would mean that the Arabs were right: there would be no hope of justice for their people except in some future military victory.

10

But for the Arabs to go on dreaming of victory would be disastrous for the ordinary people of the Middle East. Another war could involve the world.

In New York, I had read an edifying piece by the great Jewish intellectual editor of *Stone's Weekly*, I. F. Stone, in the August 3rd *New York Review of Books*.

He had written, on June 12th, 1967:

"Israel's swift and brilliant victory only makes its reconciliation with the Arabs more urgent. Its future, and world peace call for a general and final settlement of the Palestine problem. The cornerstone of that settlement must be to find new homes for the Arab refugees, some within Israel, some outside it, all with compensation for their lost lands and properties."

In a *New York Review* article just off the press, for this was still July, he wrote:

"The path to safety and the path to greatness lies in reconciliation. The other route, now that the West Bank and Gaza are under Israeli jurisdiction, leads to new perils. The Arab population now in the conquered territories makes guerilla war possible within Israel's own boundaries. And externally, if enmity deepens and tension rises between Israel and the Arab states, both sides will by one means or another obtain nuclear weapons for the next round."

It seemed so obvious to me that the Israeli government would see this clearly. It seemed so important that the western press should keep its readers informed on the directions being taken. It seemed so shocking that I, who had taken a special interest in the Middle East, could arrive in Amman so unprepared for what seemed to be the facts.

"Well, you can go and see for yourself tomorrow," Mr. Saleh said. "I suggest you start at the bridge."

11

three

Back to the Tents

THE BRIDGE HAD BEEN DESTROYED BUT A NARROW FOOTBRIDGE had been placed over the river. Refugees were coming eastward in a steady stream, carrying their beds and their babies with them.

Some of the elderly ones and the women with several babies and small children were being helped courteously by well armed young Israelis. No one was heading the other way.

Once across the Jordan they seemed to know where they were going. Some had old trucks waiting for them, others just took to the road without ever looking back, heading northward to the crowded camps: to those awful rock-strewn, fly-bitten, dust-laden, overflowing camps I had passed on the way.

Yet this was not the mad rush that had brought two hundred thousand tumbling through and over the river a few weeks before. They had been people fleeing in panic behind their own retreating armies and in front of Israeli tanks, away from the bombing planes and the napalm that had turned some to charcoal and had scarred others for life.

These had sat it out for six weeks and more on the other side. Then each for his own good or bad reasons had decided to leave the Occupied Territories.

Some were coming to join separated families; some were looking for lost wives and children, or to get funds, for they could no longer get money from frozen bank accounts on the West side. Some came to East Jordan so they could get mail and cheques from working members of the family living in the Gulf States. Some were in trouble with the Israelis. Some were from villages the Israelis had demolished.

Mr. Ishak Nashashibi of UNRWA took us to a big white tent surrounded by blue and green ones in a camp near the Allenby Bridge.

"These Danish ones are the best," he said. "The others, well, they are fine for the beach. They will never do for winter. One good wind . . ." and he waved goodbye.

Inside one tent a man and woman were sitting helplessly as half a bushel of potatoes rolled about their feet. He had new blankets and a new mess kit, and two small children. The faces of the children were covered with sores. Nine flies crawled on the sores of one. The children had no will or energy to brush the flies away.

I looked at Nashashibi. He turned away. "Well, at least we're feeding them," he said. "This is worse than 1948."

"It's worse because so many of them are two-time losers," a Jordanian doctor told me. "We're starting to rear a third generation in the camps, and after twenty years the camps weren't so bad. Now it's back to the tents again."

"What makes me so damned mad," the doctor told me, "is we have good camps on the other side, with clinics, a hospital, good schools, recreation grounds, trees – homes for a hundred thousand people. And most of our staff is over there. We need them here but we can't expect them to come, for the Israelis mightn't let them back later, and could confiscate everything they have as they did last time."

"Why did these poor people come and the staff stay?" I asked.

He explained that some of the staff would have been at Jerusalem and other places when the war broke out. Then, too, they were more sophisticated and less likely to panic.

"Some of these people should have stayed behind," a nurse said. "But then what do you do when the bombs and shells are falling? Some were just frightened. The Israelis are very good at frightening people they want to get rid of."

The largest concentration of refugees had lived since 1948 within a few miles of the Allenby Bridge, most of them on the

West side of the Jordan outside Jericho, but substantial numbers were on the East side at Karameh. That part of the Jordan valley is almost on a level with the Dead Sea, below sea level and very hot in summer and warm in winter.

Jericho is fertile and fruitful and the Arabs have been turning the East bank into productive farms and orchards. In the panic of war over two hundred thousand fled across and through the river and many remained in the Karameh area. I was shown the camp kitchens which were equipped to cook for twelve hundred. That day they were preparing food for thirty-two thousand.

It was estimated at the end of July 1967 that there were sixty-five thousand new refugees in camps and a hundred and fifty thousand others in caves, doubled up with relatives, making do one way or another. Most were hoping and expecting to return to the West Bank any day.

Among them were some hundreds whose homes had been demolished after the fighting to make room in East Jerusalem for devout Jews to pray at the Wailing Wall. I had a clipping in my pocket from a Toronto paper of a letter written by the Israeli Ambassador in Canada, saying the demolished homes were "hovels," and that the homeless Arabs had been provided with housing elsewhere.

"They weren't hovels," Saleh said. "They were poor but they were the homes of our people. I hadn't heard that they were given houses elsewhere. Many of them are here. I've seen them."

Actually, some compensation was later provided Arabs whose homes had been so quickly expropriated and demolished.

Saleh introduced me to one of his old friends who was a new refugee. He had been a miller in Beit Nuba, one of three border villages the Israelis had demolished – Beit Nuba, Yalu, and Emmaus.

"The Israelis first shelled the village," the old man said. "Then they moved in and ordered us all out and told us to walk toward Ramallah. Eight persons were killed. Some old people who were ill couldn't leave. They were buried alive. The Israelis said the area was declared a military zone. They demolished my mill and carted it away, but they bulldozed everything else under.

"We remained in Ramallah for two weeks, trying to get permission to go back and bury our dead," he said. "Then finally we had to come here. The Israelis provided many of us with rides to the river."

That was one of the things I found angered many refugees in retrospect – those free rides out of their country.

Saleh told me he knew many of the people from those villages. The old man, he said, was trustworthy and I could believe his story completely.

"Do you want to go back?" I asked him. Official surveys indicate that well over ninety per cent of the Palestinians wished to return, and when they fled they had assumed they could go back when the trouble was over. "I'd go back even if I had to sit under a tree," he said. He had formerly owned a twelve-room stone house and was a man of some stature in Beit Nuba.

Later, in Israel, I asked the press representative at the Foreign Ministry if I could be taken to Beit Nuba, Yalu, and Emmaus. She said I couldn't go. So I put in a formal request to go to Beit Nuba. She had been very co-operative, but shook her head. A young man was brought. "You can't go," he said. "Why not?" I asked. "There isn't any Beit Nuba." He explained that it and some other border villages had been demolished as a threat to the security of the airport. He added that fedayeen had been housed there, so I wasn't sure whether it was a military security measure or a reprisal. Whatever it was, it made some thousands homeless.

Sister Marie Therese, a French missionary, described Beit Nuba later in June 1967 when she and some other Arabic-speaking missionaries managed to elude the Israeli guards and visit the sites of the villages.

In *Jerusalem et le Sang les Pauvres* she wrote:

"And there was what the Israelis did not want us to see; three villages systematically destroyed by dynamite and bulldozers. Alone in a deathly silence donkeys wandered about the ruins. Here and there a crushed piece of furniture

15

or a torn pillow stuck out of the mass of plaster, stones and concrete."

One of the horror stories being told in Amman was of the experiences of fleeing refugees being sprayed with napalm. At first I didn't believe it and shuddered at the thought of using some of the pictures of victims available in Jordan.

"If it were about Vietnam you'd publish them wouldn't you?" a Palestinian said.

General Sir John Glubb, in his interpretation of The Middle East Crisis published in July 1967 and frequently reprinted, states:

"The greater part of the Jordan army were destroyed by napalm. . . ."

He quotes from a signed statement from a team of doctors of the American University of Beirut who volunteered to help in Jordan military hospitals:

"I handled 600 to 700 patients of whom 160 were civilians. Two hundred were suffering from secondary degree burns. I did not see a single bullet wound."

"Many soldiers say that their units were destroyed by fire without their ever seeing an Israeli soldier."

"A doctor reported that the Mobile Field Hospital, containing 350 patients, was incinerated with all its patients and staff by napalm," Glubb says.

Israel tried to keep the outside world from knowing about their quiet, effective use of napalm, and Zionists abroad denied it. But some of the living victims were in an Amman hospital.

Mr. Saleh was very upset about Mr. Sami Oweida, a Jericho official who remained at his post until the afternoon of July 7th, then gave in to the pleas of his family and left for the East Bank. I decided to interview Mr. Oweida, but he spoke only Arabic. Later I got a translation of his transcribed story.

16

"We left at 2:30 P.M. on Wednesday, and on the way to the bridge saw about 200 bodies of soldiers and civilians. . . . We crossed the King Hussein [Allenby] Bridge, walking. Planes were going overhead. . . . We tried to avoid big crowds, thinking the planes would bomb the crowds.

"Then at that moment [about 4 P.M.] I saw a plane come down like a hawk directly at us. We threw ourselves on the ground and found ourselves in the midst of fire. Children were on fire. Myself, my two daughters, my son, and two children of my cousin. I tried to do something but in vain. Fire was all around. I carried my burning child outside the fire. The burning people became naked. Fire stuck to my hands and face. I rolled over. The fire rolled with me.

"I saw another plane coming directly at us. I thought it was the end. I saw the pilot lean over and look at me.

"My daughter, Kabiba [four years old], died that night. Two children of my cousin also died. My daughter Adla, seventeen years old, died four days later."

The Oweidas were still in hospital. When I went to Jerusalem later I had pictures of them, I am not sure why, with a lot of other film. I showed some of them to a travel agent in East Jerusalem with whom I was arranging transport to Bethlehem. His name was transliterated as "Aweidah." "My God," he exclaimed when he saw the pictures, "that's my nephew from Jericho. My niece begged me to go to Amman too. But I was a refugee before and decided not to go this time." He looked at the pictures again – of nephews and nieces and cousins, civilians who had fled from Jericho and had been napalmed from the air.

I wished I had stuck to the business of going to Bethlehem and hadn't shown pictures from the other side.

Later I did publish one of the pictures in the *United Church Observer*, of a little girl recovering from napalm burns. That, I was told, proved I was anti-Semitic. To condemn napalm in Vietnam is alright. To report its use by the Israelis is considered anti-Semitic.

four

A Night
in the Worst Camp in the World

ON MY WAY THROUGH BEIRUT I EXPLAINED TO MISS RUTH
Black, veteran refugee worker for the World Council of
Churches, that I wanted "to get the feel of this refugee thing."
She looked me over and said, "Okay, go to Wadi Dleel. It's
the worst situation I have ever seen – probably the worst refu-
gee camp in the world."

Wadi Dleel means "Valley of the Lost." During the summer
of 1967 the Jordan Government organized and operated an
emergency food and shelter programme there for about thirteen thousand refugees who continued to cross the Jordan after
the fighting of June ended.

When I told Shukri Saleh I'd like to go to Wadi Dleel and
spend the night he gave me a funny look.

That summer anti-Americanism hadn't appeared in the way
it did later, but it still wasn't recommended that persons who
looked as American as I did go wandering around refugee
camps during the night.

We arrived in mid-afternoon. About three thousand tents
were pitched among the boulders in the dust of the valley. It
was dust, not sand. The tents were in neat rows. Boulders had
been lined up to separate the tents and mark foot paths. Some
of the people had chickens, some goats, and a few had planted
tiny gardens. Give them time, I thought, and they will turn
even this awful place into an Arab village.

When the wind blew the dust swirled, settling on the faces
of the children like flour from a mill. There were about seven

thousand children in Wadi Dleel. There were a few fathers, a lot of mothers. The nurses in the British Save the Children Fund clinic in the corner of the camp where I made my home told me they estimated three-quarters of the women were pregnant.

Where were the fathers? They had not deserted, but war separates. Some had been killed. Some were prisoners of war. Some were in the underground. Some were in hiding. Others were working in Kuwait and Saudi Arabia or Libya, and that was why the families had come to the East Bank. They couldn't get mail or money on the other side after the Israeli occupation.

Others were just lost, and in time the divided families would locate the missing ones. Some were sitting it out on the other side, waiting to get their families back home. If they came to Wadi Dleel to fetch them they mightn't ever get home again.

Mr. Saleh took me to the young Jordanian officer who was in charge, to ask permission for me to remain the night. The officer was courteous and embarrassed but wouldn't grant it. He explained he was thinking of my safety only. But he didn't say I couldn't. He just wasn't going to accept the responsibility such permission implied. I got the impression from Mr. Saleh that if I kept out of sight and didn't start a riot I'd be all right.

I asked the Save the Children people if they had a spare cot in a spare tent. Dr. Cecile Ackere, a Belgian doctor, said I could have her folding cot in the provision tent if I liked.

She suggested I might make myself useful after dark by guarding the provisions. She said there wasn't much pilfering, but in a camp of thirteen thousand people who had lost their homes and most of their belongings and weren't getting enough to eat, it was a good idea to have a guard. I was flattered.

Dr. Ackere was busy. "We do have lots of water," she said. "That's why the camp is here. It's the only good thing about it." I hung around her clinic while she closed down for the medical day. "The children are always stubbing their toes or falling over stones and cutting themselves," she said. "I am afraid of serious infection so I shoot penicillin into them. I've never shot so much penicillin into people in my life." Dr. Ackere worked among refugee children in the Congo and in southern Jordan for many years. She knew how to inject penicillin. At the Wadi she had a special reason.

When I arrived in the late afternoon I wondered why so many of the campers were wandering away out on the desert behind the camp. Then I learned the place had no latrines; thirteen thousand people had not a single latrine. "The desert is your bathroom," one of the Arab male nurses with the SCF told me.

Many of the children and some of the adults didn't make the desert; I was advised again to watch my step. Flies infested the place. That was one of the reasons Dr. Ackere kept the penicillin going.

The heat and the dust and the flies, the overcrowding, the inadequate and imbalanced diet – all threatened the medical people in Jordan. "It's a miracle we haven't had an epidemic," one senior doctor told me.

Just behind my little tent was the kitchen – another tent. A long line of children got their supplies from UNRWA and emergency government stores, but the SCF supplemented the feeding for the children with a ladle of cooked rice and lentils covered with sour milk.

An astonishing number of the children could speak a little English, learned in their UNRWA schools in the camps from which they had fled. Like children everywhere they were friendly to a friendly stranger. They seemed an attractive and not unhappy lot.

(When Mary Hawkins of the British SCF, a veteran worker among the Palestine refugees, arrived the next morning, she told me that many of the children were the offspring of children she had helped look after nineteen years before on the West Bank of the Jordan, when their parents were first made refugees by the partition of Palestine and the subsequent Israeli expansion. She had personally registered seven thousand children since the June war and that included eleven hundred she had signed in during a seven day period at the end of July.)

Two English nurses, Audrey Brunt and Anne Broadbent, operated a clinic for mothers and small babies in one of the sweltering tents. Some of the babies had been born since the mothers arrived; some had been delivered by the roadside as the mothers fled.

"A mother with new-born twins came walking in the other day," Miss Brunt told me. "They had been born by the side of the road. We got them to a hospital."

"And a little girl of about twelve came in with a baby whose mother had died with a miscarriage during her flight. We showed the child how to care for the infant, but I was afraid the baby would die," Miss Broadbent said. "I guess it did," she added thoughtfully. "I just realized she has not been back." There were too many babies that chaotic summer for even the most efficient and dedicated people to save.

The nurses closed their clinic in late afternoon and went back to SCF headquarters in Amman to eat and sleep. Dr. Ackere settled down in her clinic to work on her day's records. I wandered about.

As the end of the feeding line came for the children and the last of them went off with their tins of rice and lentils, to share with brothers and sisters back in the tents, it was suddenly dark.

I was beginning to get hungry and questioned Ruth Black's whole idea of staying the night. I could have used some of that rice and sour milk myself but it was all gone. Food, I suspected, didn't interest Dr. Ackere much. But suddenly she remembered me and felt an obligation to the guest left on her hands. So we rummaged about and found some Arab bread and sausage, but no knife to cut the sausage. Oh well! We broke off some hunks. There was cheese. There was some powdered milk. And there were fresh grapes.

We brushed the dust off a rickety table and spread our food and adjusted the smokey lamp so we could see. "This is very nutritious," Dr. Ackere said with a smile.

I have eaten at the Waldorf – once. And at London's Savoy – twice. But that simple meal was more memorable; I shall never forget it or my gracious hostess. We did not linger long. Dr. Ackere had a great pile of medical records to write up so I helped put away the food. Long after I had blown out my own smokey lamp in the tent next door I could see her shadow bent over the table and those records.

It was too early for me to go to sleep and I could hear a murmur of Arab voices in a tent on my other side, where the Arab male nurses who helped in the clinics and the food distribution were sleeping. They gave me the customary "Welcome" when I slipped into their tent.

They had been refugees almost all their lives and told me how each had been a small boy when his parents lost their homes in 1948.

"There will be war again," one said and the rest agreed. I argued. Did they want to do to the young people of Israel what had been done to them – "throw them into the sea" as some of their leaders had threatened?

"That was a foolish thing to say," one replied. "We wish no harm to the ordinary Israeli people but Zionism will have to go. What else can we do? They have taken our homes and land and the United Nations said we can go back but the Zionists will not let us back. Now they have expanded again, and you will see they will keep what they have taken despite the UN."

"What do you think we should do?" one asked me, and I didn't have too much to say. I went back after awhile to my tent and guarded the supplies but none of the thirteen thousand seemed interested in what I was guarding.

They rose before the sun in Wadi Dleel and the sun rose early. I was wakened by the chattering of hundreds of little children and peeked out my tent to see them lined up again with their registration cards and tin mugs for breakfast.

Miss Hawkins had arrived too, a wiry and peppery little woman, fresh from her bath and sleep in a bed and with a hair-do. About four hundred more refugees had arrived during the night and in the early morning and were lined up to register with her.

I raided the kitchen for some breakfast and wandered about, trying to keep out of the way of busy people. The mothers and babies were filling the nurses' tent. Dr. Ackere was already receiving older children and shooting in the penicillin. One of the Arab nurses was splashing water about to lay the dust in the clinic. He spilled a little and it turned to sticky mud.

22

Miss Hawkins later had a brief coffee break with me and explained how the SCF worked. She obviously knew how to handle the press and answered every question – her sizzling comments on the Israeli and Arab establishments would have been enough to hang her in either Tel Aviv or Amman, if anyone would have dared lay a hand on that little Englishwoman.

"You need a woman here," she said, explaining how she put up with no nonsense from anyone, including the Arab refugee women. "A man couldn't touch them," she said, "or they would scream for the police, or the husband would come looking for a fight. But I can."

"You'll see no depression among these women despite what they have gone through and are going through. It was different in the refugee camps of Europe after the war where I worked. We had our suicides there, but never here. Whatever happens they say it is the will of Allah. That is their trouble and their salvation. It makes me so angry when a child that might have been saved with proper medical attention dies and they say it is the will of Allah. On the other hand they accept the things they cannot change with a shrug and 'Inshallah.' "

A little later in the day I went back to Amman; the wealthy people of the city were bringing their children to the hotel to swim in the pool for the afternoon – indifferent it seemed to me to the seven thousand youngsters in the dusty desert to the north and the tens of thousands more in chaotic Jordan. They were doing, of course, what I and my children would be doing back home.

Since that night I have often seen the Save the Children people at their work and, although professionally my first loyalty is to my church and I remain an enthusiast for the people who work for the UN and its agencies and believe they should be supported generously, I am a convert to the SCF. I have met no more competent, dedicated, or civilized people anywhere than those great women whom I met at Wadi Dleel.

A short time later Wadi Dleel was closed and its refugees were sent to other permanent camps operated by UNRWA. "We've agreed to take it over," Mr. Laurence Michelmore, head of UNRWA, told me at breakfast one August morning in Damascus, "but not in that place."

23

And so, for a short time in that mad summer of 1967, an emergency government camp, dubbed by some "the worst in the world," gave shelter to the thousands in their desperation. Most of those people are still in the Jordanian camps. Most of those seven thousand will grow up to be homeless Palestinians just as their parents were. Although they were hoping and expecting to return to the West Bank of the Jordan that summer, only a few of them got back.

five

How Egypt Cared
for the New Refugees

A LITTLE LAD KEPT PLUCKING AT MY ARM AND LOOKING UP, trying to get something said, while older men crowded round and talked excitedly.

"There was a lot of bombing and shooting, and people were getting killed; everybody was running, and I was afraid I was going to get killed too. So I ran," an Arab of about twenty-five explained.

He was trying to make me understand why he was away over in an Egyptian village that had been converted into a refugee camp in the UAR Liberation province half-way between Cairo and Alexandria, and he didn't know where his wife and children were. He said he too had been a refugee for nineteen years, ever since his parents fled to Gaza in the 1948 war.

Finally the little boy had his chance. He thought I was from the Red Cross, he said, and asked, "Are you going to Gaza?" I said I might. The interpreter explained. "He wants you to please tell his mother if you get to Gaza that he didn't get killed. He's here."

So I had him write down his name and his mother's name and address, and then others wrote down their names and the names of their families in Gaza. And the camp director looked at his watch and said this was the first stop in the first camp and there were eight other camps. He might have suggested that we didn't have all day and there were a lot of other kids who had got separated from their mothers and I wasn't working for the Red Cross anyway.

25

So I went on.

Two days later in Damascus I took that little boy's name and address to the International Red Cross representative to discuss getting messages from lost little boys to their mothers. He shook his head. "We've got fourteen thousand letters piled up here from Syrian displaced persons and we can't get censors to go through them." He was sympathetic, as I always find the Red Cross to be – and they would work on it. But there were other things – food, medicine, shelter, politics – that had to come first.

I did get to Gaza. But there were over four hundred thousand people jammed into Gaza in that narrow strip between the desert and Israel and the sea, over three hundred thousand of them refugees. It was and is the worst situation in the Middle East.

I was unable to let the lad's mother know he hadn't been killed. I carried the address in my pocket and about fifteen months later I went back to the Liberation Province and returned to the same camp and the same hut. Most of them were still there. They remembered me and they remembered the boy.

"He's in Alexandria with his father," I was told. "His mother is in Gaza and it is unlikely they will get together, but she knows now he didn't get killed."

The Red Cross told me that Egyptian radio did a good job with this sort of thing, broadcasting lists of names of people who had disappeared but hadn't been killed and had turned up as refugees in the UAR. The problem was that there was no way to let the refugees know if the messages got through.

Although the UAR had suffered a disastrous and humiliating defeat and had lost the Gaza Strip (which was really not UAR territory but had been under her administration) and the whole of the Sinai, her refugee problem was less acute than that in Jordan and Syria.

About a hundred and thirty thousand Syrians and Palestinians had fled from the Golan Heights. About two hundred and fifteen thousand at that time had crossed the Jordan. About thirty-five thousand from Gaza and Sinai, most of them former Palestinian refugees, but a substantial number of Sinai

Bedouins too, had become guests on the West side of Suez.

It was obvious Egypt was trying to do a good job, although the Palestinians didn't like it and wanted to go back. Many Egyptians weren't very pleased at their presence.

"They won't work," the UAR camp director told me. "There's work here in the fields and we'll pay them, but they are afraid if they start to work they will be kept here and never get back to their families." An angry Palestinian kept following us as he showed me about the camp. "He keeps saying he wants to go back to Gaza," the director explained.

About ten thousand were crowded into new villages in the Liberation Province; the houses were all filled and so were the new schools. At one time in Jordan there were as many as thirty families in a school-room. In the UAR schools each family had a corner of a school-room.

Although UNRWA had made arrangements quickly to continue providing rations for the UNRWA refugees, the UAR was paying cash instead of distributing food. Each person was given the equivalent of about twenty-five cents a day up to two and a half dollars for a large family. A farm labourer was paid about one dollar a day. You could buy a dozen eggs or a big watermelon for about twenty-five cents.

One of the ironies was that the new villages in the Province had been planned and built for young families from Upper Egypt. The UAR has a vast reclamation project in the delta and had already reclaimed about one hundred thousand acres from the desert. Eventually they will reclaim a million. The fields were producing alfalfa, citruses, vegetables, and grains.

I was given an excellent lunch of both chicken and steak in the headquarters building dining room. The good things were all grown right there, I was told with pride. It was significant that there was a bowl of fresh roses on every dining room table. The Egyptians make roses grow in the desert too, and they have reclaimed approximately the same acreage that Israel has during recent years.

"But you didn't know about it did you?" my host said. "Why don't your journalists write about this too?"

When the refugees flooded in after the June war the government postponed the movement of young families from the south to the new homes and fields they had been waiting for, and housed the refugees in the villages. This was a matter of great disappointment and some resentment. The overpopulation of Egypt is serious and young Egyptians have a lot of hope for their economic and social revolution. The villages seemed well planned. Each had its Mosque and school and clinic.

Despite the problems of Egypt it seemed then that the refugee problem would be taken in stride. Subsequently, arrangements were worked out with the Red Cross to reunite many of the families. While Israel permitted no Syrians to return to their homes even for the most pressing compassionate reasons – except a few hundred Druses – most of the divided Sinai and Gaza families were reunited. In time Egypt made arrangements with UNRWA to look after all the Palestinians for whom UNRWA had responsibility.

Not many would have predicted then that the UAR problem of displaced persons had just begun. In the two years to follow over a half a million of their own people were to be driven from the West bank of the Suez Canal by Israeli shells and bombs, and the large cities of Suez and Ismailia were emptied and their residents scattered all over the crowded nation.

six

In Syria the Suffering
Has Been Greatest

I HAD THOUGHT IT WAS BAD IN JORDAN. IN SOUTHERN SYRIA ten thousand refugees were sleeping in open fields. They were still fleeing from their villages as the Israeli Occupation settled in.

When I took my story of the lonely little boy from Gaza to the representative of the International Red Cross in Damascus, he told me his troubles.

"I'm screaming to Geneva for tents, real tents, real army tents. These beach tents, you can read through them; you could eat cheese through them. Thousands haven't even got tents." He complained that the western world was indifferent to Syria because it was said to be "socialist."

The Rev. James Caven, an American Presbyterian missionary, had been concentrating on the refugee situation in Damascus and hadn't been to the southern area where the Red Cross, Red Crescent, and UNRWA were working with the Syrian government to do what they could for the masses around Darragh.

We headed for Darragh and Lake Mzerib. About a hundred families were camped in the prettiest site I had seen for refugees in all my travels. A few had tents. Some had spread blankets over branches they broke from willow trees to cover their few possessions. While we were there some of the women and children were busy erecting new shelters from branches and leaves.

"We are from Galilee," they told me. A mother with a new-

29

born baby was pleased when I took a picture of the child. "He was born under a tree," she said with pride and a little humour. That baby, I thought, may have to grow up under a tree.

Under a leafy shelter nearby a young mother, not noticing me and my intruding camera, played with a baby. She nuzzled its face against her own. When the baby gurgled, she laughed softly. I hid my camera, embarrassed, and hurried away.

Children and women in long heavy peasant clothing gathered about until an angry husband arrived, not to protest our cameras or conversation, but to order his wife to fetch more water from the lake. "It's just like home," they seemed to say to us. Some other men arrived and spoke impatiently to the Red Crescent representative who accompanied us. They wanted more food, more blankets and tents.

The refugees at Mzerib discussed no politics and there were indications they had little knowledge of what it was all about. They weren't as eager to go back home as the refugees in Jordan and the UAR were. In Egypt I was told "everyone wants to go back," and I gathered the same from my conversation with them. The same was true in Jordan. Eventually, when arrangements were completed for the Jordanians to fill out application forms, a hundred and seventy thousand of the two hundred and fifteen thousand there applied to go back.

But the Syrians said, "We want to go back but under certain conditions." Caven and I asked, "What conditions?" They always answered, "That the Israelis get out."

"We've got to get these people into decent shelter before winter," the Red Cross, UNRWA, and the Church people all told me. "They will die if they don't. It gets cold here you know."

I was lucky in Damascus. Mr. Laurence Michelmore of UNRWA was visiting Syria and stayed in the New Omayad Hotel while I was there. He shared breakfast with me early one morning. That day the International Red Cross representative returned from the Allenby Bridge where he had arranged for an agreement to be signed by which the Jordanian refugees could return to the West Bank. He was jubilant. By this time I was so involved that I was jubilant too.

It turned out not to be such good news after all, for the Israelis managed, with one obstruction after another, to let back only fourteen thousand of the hundred and seventy thousand who applied to return.

The Red Cross and others were worried about the Syrians, though. Officials in Syria, including the international representatives, knew that Syrian problems weren't likely to inspire the compassion of the western world. For one thing, the country had had about twenty changes of government in recent decades and could have another coup, assassination, or upset at any moment.

There were no guarantees that supplies sent for refugees mightn't end up feeding the army. Christians couldn't send special gifts to Christians. "They are all Syrians," officials said logically. If that seemed frustrating to donors who had been used to picking and choosing the objects of their charity, it should also be said that there was almost no black market in Syria and no sign of profiteering. This couldn't be claimed in all the Arab world.

About seventeen thousand of those who had fled the Golan Heights were Palestinians from 1948, and they were cared for by UNRWA. The other hundred and twenty thousand or so were given direct relief by the government. Most of the peasant people were Moslems and were sheltered in camps. About twenty-five hundred or more Christians from Kuneitra went directly to Damascus and headed for their churches. The Catholics were housed in Catholic schools, the Protestants in the Protestant Church and school, the Orthodox in their schools.

On the whole the Christians from Kuneitra were better educated and more well-to-do than the Moslem peasants. They lost everything too, unless they were fortunate enough to have savings in a Damascus bank.

One of the ironies was that almost all the funds contributed by the World Council of Churches went to Moslems and the Christians received practically no help. Their fellow Christians in Damascus were generous but many of them were poor.

I was curious why I almost never found Christian refugees in the camps; they always seemed to make it somehow on their own in the towns and cities. There are a number of reasons for this. For one thing, Christians do not want to have their daughters in camps where they might become intimate with Moslem

31

boys – which for an Arab family is a disgrace and the end of the girl's world.

The Christians tend to be found in trade and the higher skills and professions. They are better off financially and better educated. I was told it was because, being a minority, they had to try harder and that Christians put a higher value on education.

There was another reason. For long periods in the past in the Ottoman Empire Christians were not permitted to own land in Palestine and Syria, so they acquired those skills needed to survive in the towns and emphasized education. The churches had all had schools.

In Lebanon there are old UNRWA camps of Christians but among the new refugees and in Syria and Jordan I found no Christians in the camps.

A Syrian taxi-driver, who told me he didn't think much of the government and didn't know anybody who did, drove me over the moutains to Beirut. He confided that he sometimes wished the Israelis had taken Damascus too, and then they might have got rid of the government. You get that from more people than taxi-drivers in Syria.

He asked if I minded sharing the taxi with some border officials. "I keep in good with them by giving them rides. That way I never have trouble," he explained.

At the Syrian-Lebanon frontier he took my passport and told me to stay put. I signed no papers, paid no money. We went on through. I did have time to count eighty-six big transports waiting their turn to pass through customs, most of them transporting supplies to the refugees in Jordan for UNRWA and the government.

"How did you get me through without more fuss?" I asked. He said, "I told them you were a big shot working for the Red Cross. Right now the Red Cross is in good here. Next week I might tell them you were UN, or World Council of Churches, or whatever is in good then. I sure didn't tell them you were an editor or we would have had to sit there for hours."

Beirut looked pleasant. The Lebanese in their way had managed to stay out of the war or they most certainly would have lost the south of Lebanon and had a new refugee problem too.

Lebanon has a hundred and seventy thousand registered Palestinian refugees from 1948, about forty per cent of them in camps. Many hundreds of Palestine students were marooned at schools and colleges and they were not permitted to go back to their homes. The American University of Beirut, the YMCA and YWCA and other organizations sustained the students during the emergency. They created a significant political focus of anti-Israeli protest and still do. While there was frustration and unhappiness and uncertainty, the suffering to be found in Syria and on the West Bank was not evident.

seven

Triumphant Israel—1967

IN AUGUST OF 1967 CYPRUS WAS ALREADY BEGINNING TO prosper with the new traffic of two-passport passengers from Cairo and Beirut to Tel Aviv and back. Immigration officials were sophisticated about it all and still are.

I passed through Nicosia on my way to one of those red-carpet welcomes for which Israel is famous when meeting journalists.

One day back in July I had telephoned a Zionist official in Toronto to get some information for a piece I was writing for a book on "Religion in Canada." We were good friends and I told him I was going to Israel later in the summer. Within the hour there was a telephone call from the Israeli Ambassador in Ottawa, His Excellency Mr. Gershon Avner, who wanted to help. Local Zionists had always kept an eye on the *Observer*, especially when a staff member made trips to the Middle East. Their papers usually reprinted any nice things we might say about Israel and any critical comments we might make about Arabs. Through the years my contact with the Canadian Arab community had been nil.

Mr. Avner was most solicitous; he sent along a copy of a letter of introduction he had written to Israeli officials, saying I was a fine friend of Israel and so on. Arrangements were made for me to be met at the Lod airport and shown about. I chose my own hotel and paid my own way and was grateful for the opportunity to see several Israeli officials, including Mr. Michael Comay, former ambassador to Canada and to the UN and later ambassador to London.

Mr. Comay is an exceptionally gracious person. I told him what I had seen at the Allenby Bridge and in the refugee camps. He seemed to be completely candid with me and shared my concern for the refugees.

He was working hard, he said, to make arrangements to let the refugees back. "But it is becoming politically very difficult," he explained.

The Jordanians had instructed the refugees, "Go back and be a thorn in the side of Israel." The Israeli people had all heard this on the radio and didn't want them back.

"We can't afford to risk the condemnation of the world again," Mr. Comay said. "I can assure you we will do everything possible to unite families and return them to their homes." I was much impressed with Mr. Comay. I said, "If you don't let those poor people back I am going to hit it as hard as I can." He smiled and said, "Well, you're an editor and that's your job."

He explained, "Some people think we just can't handle all the new territory, but militarily we are much better off than we were before. Look at our borders now." He emphasized that Israel didn't want the Sinai. "It's a good buffer between us and the Egyptians." But he said Jerusalem would be kept as one city and the capital of Israel, and often referred to King David of three thousand years before. "No government in Israel would survive if we didn't hold Jerusalem."

As for Syria and the Golan Heights, "Syria is impossible. What have they had, twenty governments in twenty-two years or something? We can settle half a million people on those heights."

He told me of Israel's great plans for the West Bank. A team of experts had been appointed to study the economic, social, and agricultural problems of the area, and if I were to come back in a year or so I would find the Arabs who remained behind would be much more prosperous.

He admitted some concern for the Gaza Strip but he predicted that they would do a lot better than the Egyptians had done and suggested that some of the Gaza people were happier to be with Israel than with the UAR. He also implied that there weren't nearly as many refugees as UNRWA claimed and that Israel was going to have a thorough census. He agreed I should go to see Gaza and told me not to go on a Saturday, that the highways were jammed with so many Israelis going to Gaza to buy up black market materials left by the Egyptians.

I liked Michael Comay and most of the other Israelis I met from the Foreign Ministry and the press. But I also had contacts in East Jerusalem and with Arabs in Occupied Jordan and I didn't get quite the same story, although in 1967 there was not the Arab bitterness against Israel that was soon to develop in Occupied Jordan.

One thing I wanted was to go to the Allenby Bridge and see it from the Israeli side, and to see that paper all the Arabs who left were forced to sign before leaving. It took some days, for the Defense Minister had ordered, "Nobody, but nobody, to the bridge." Eventually I got there late one afternoon. I didn't see much – just a few Arabs going East; none coming West. The paper was a simple document stating that they were leaving of their own free will. Actually, it signed away their birthright; those who signed it did not and will not get back.

I found some of my Palestinian friends from other years very bitter. Others admitted they were fed up with King Hussein and the Palestine Liberation Organization anyway and thought it might be better under Israel.

"I was a refugee once," one of them told me. "But I have a good little business and five children and I made up my mind I wasn't going to be a refugee again. I have always been able to get along and do business with Jews. I think I can again. They are smart. They fought a smart war. I'm going to try to get along." Fifteen months later he was to tell me, "I can't make a living for my children. Everybody hates them now".

I went to Jericho and the empty camps. Most of the shops in Jericho were closed and most of the houses were empty. The camps which had sheltered over sixty-five thousand Palestinians had been completely emptied. School books were scattered about. The people had gone in a hurry.

In the centre of one of the big camps I found a few families who told me they had fled to the other side but within a few days had waded back across the river and returned home. "The Israelis know we are here, but they don't bother us," I was told. It was rather lonely for a dozen or so Arabs to be living in ghost camps.

36

One of the most striking things about Israel was the change in the attitude of the young people since my visit in February 1967. Then I had found them complaining about taxes and the government and the unemployment and especially the influence of the rabbinate.

By August 1967, they were proud, and some rather arrogant, nationalists. They had fought a quick war and won it brilliantly. Most of them were convinced that their backs were to the sea and that if they had lost they would have been destroyed as a nation and as individuals. They had had brilliant leadership and they had done their bit.

The Arabs had been boastful and stupid and while there was some pity for "the poor refugees," there wasn't much. "It served them right for following Shukeiry and Nasser," they would say.

I stayed in the Holy Land Hotel outside the new Israeli city. It was easy to make friends. The guests soon came to know I was a Canadian interested in the aftermath of this war, especially the refugees. There were calls and cars from the Foreign Ministry, and an Israeli television crew worked with me for a CBC film the CBC never showed.

Each evening I would be invited to join some group or other and I would tell them what I had seen and what I thought and they would tell me what they thought. They were good people, eager to tell me how some of their best friends were Arabs.

But sometimes one would argue black was white. I had been in the old city one afternoon and seen where a shell had entered a certain home. I was to take back pictures of the damage to a Canadian son of the family to assure him that despite the damage everything would be all right. I mentioned that. An Israeli guest argued it was just not so: no Israeli shells had hit that part of the city. The same was said when I mentioned the Augusta Victoria hospital. I must not believe what I had seen.

I was surprised that even in Israel good people were victims of their own propaganda.

eight

What Happened
When I Criticized Israel

IN THE MONTHS THAT FOLLOWED THE PUBLICATION OF MY reports on the refugee situation in the Middle East I was subjected to a barrage of innuendo and invective.

In thirty years of more or less public church life, fifteen of them editing the largest – and I like to think in some ways one of the most respected – church paper in the British Commonwealth, I had never known anything like it. One cannot take a place as a responsible editor in the free church press without angering some people. There is usually a way in which controversy can be carried on with decency. However, I have found no way to criticize the policies of the State of Israel, or question the philosophy of political Zionism, or tell my readers what the facts of the Middle East are, and escape slander and libel from the Zionist-Israeli community. In Israel it is different.

During one period of bitter attack on me I asked Pierre Berton, Canada's ablest – and I suppose most controversial – author, editor, and television personality, about it. Berton and fellow broadcaster, Charles Templeton, had come to my defense on a programme when I had been called an anti-Semite for criticizing Israel. Berton had an impeccable record as a friend to the Jews and other minorities. I thought I had, too.

"Why are they zeroing in on me?" I asked him. "Many have been more critical of Israel and less critical of the Arabs than I have."

"It's because you keep on the refugee problem," he said.

"Every Jew in the world feels guilty about that. It's when you criticize people where their guilt complexes are that you get such a reaction."

In New York, on my way back to Toronto, I spent a day with some of my editors, Janet Harbison and Karl Karsch of *Presbyterian Life*, Henry McCorkle of the *Episcopalian*, and Martin Bailey of the *United Church Herald*. They de-briefed me and criticized my photography. The editors were shocked at the pictures of napalmed victims and it was decided by several that they wouldn't print them. Despite the evidence we couldn't quite expect the public to believe that Israel had actually napalmed civilian refugees.

It was obvious to me that the church press was interested chiefly in telling the story of "the poor refugees," and moving church-goers to express their compassion on the collection plate. A dozen or so church publications soon carried my reports. In Canada I did a six-part syndicated series for the *Toronto Star*. I was interviewed on a number of radio and television programmes.

After my pieces began to appear I received a letter from Bill Gottleib, of the American Council of Judaism, with a warning: "Unless I miss my guess there will be some kind of public outcry from Zionists and you may as well be prepared for all kinds of slanderous charges." He said that statements such as I had made "rarely appear in the American press" and thanked me.

It just hadn't occurred to me that anyone would ever charge me or the *United Church Observer* with being racist, or bigoted, or, of all things, anti-Semitic. Occasionally I had been surprised in the past to hear such charges levelled at others whom I had respected. But usually I assumed there had been a misunderstanding – or maybe, just maybe, there had been reasons. We had our faults and we had made our mistakes in the *Observer* and had been taken apart by those who disagreed with us, but never had there been any hint or any grounds for a hint that we would descend to racism. My professional and personal relations with the Jewish community were excellent. I counted as my friends the leading rabbis of my city. I had never hesitated to disagree or agree with them on public issues. To me, as it is to most liberal Christians, anti-Semitism has always been one of the viler sins – the sort of thing stupid, sick, or ignorant people might be guilty of. Just look at the fruits of anti-Semitism in Germany!

But I was wrong.

"Monstrous allegations and falsehoods," the *Canadian Zionist* thundered. "If he decides to carry on his one man war against Israel he must accept the consequences. . . ." A Guelph, Ontario, rabbi wrote the *Mercury,* "Biased views completely unsupported by facts."

Toronto's leading rabbi, a long-time personal friend, asked for space to reply. I provided it. He wrote a forthright criticism which we published in the *Observer* without comment. Although I was surprised at the propaganda clichés he repeated, I thought he was sincere. He did not descend to name calling.

The Israeli Ambassador demanded I publish a letter which turned out to be nearly four thousand words long. I insisted he cut it, for it looked as though I were going to have to devote an issue to rebuttals, some of which were slanderous and personal.

He charged that I had "made a scurrilous attack on Israel," and had been an inveterate opponent of the State of Israel since before 1948. He suggested I turned "the *Observer* into an adjunct of the Arab League Propaganda Office in Ottawa." I didn't know there was one.

I was surprised at the 1948 charge about "vicious one-sided propaganda," as he called it, for I had written nothing about Israel until the mid-fifties and then it was – to me as I re-read it now – embarrassingly pro-Israeli. It seemed strange from him, for a few weeks before he had been writing fulsome stuff to the Israeli officials, saying I was a friend of Israel and a distinguished leader of the Canadian Anglican Church. Well, I'm not an Anglican but that, I suppose, could be overlooked.

"We have a file on you and it goes back twenty years," John Devor, a leading Toronto Zionist, said to me, wagging his finger. Devor found out later, when he checked, that the file was on the *Observer,* and my distinguished predecessor had written an editorial at the time Israel came into being that regretted that the Jewish people hadn't been ready to settle for a home without having a religious state. It made sense. But

I didn't write it and at the time I was a very obscure and, I like to think, rather youthful pastor.

"We heard the Arab League mailed out fifty thousand copies of that issue of the *Observer*," John Devor told me. Actually, the Arab League had bought some of the overrun and mailed out two hundred copies.

In the *Globe Magazine*, Toronto, Myrer Sharzer, a Jewish Congress official, was quoted as calling me a "dupe of Communist and Arab propaganda." Sharzer wrote immediately to say he hadn't said "Communist"; I was just a dupe of the Arabs. I suggested he owed the explanation to the readers of the *Globe*, and he eventually made it. It was a rather tortured explanation, saying that the author who quoted him – who as time went on I noted was a very pro-Israeli writer named Oliver Clausen – was a splendid reporter, but that wasn't exactly what he meant. Clausen told me he was sure it was.

While this was building up, some "friends" were beginning to say, "I don't think he is an anti-Semite." Rabbi Emil Fackenheim of the University of Toronto demanded in the papers that I be removed from the chairmanship of a teach-in panel at the University of Toronto. The *Toronto Telegram*, which is pro-Zionist to a point that should embarrass the people on its staff with an IQ, editorialized that I should be removed. That got attention. I was reproved but not removed.

A little later I was participating as a special speaker at a student "religions" week at the University of Winnipeg. Some local lady called the president and demanded I be struck from the programme. When he protested she shouted that he was "a bigoted anti-Semite" and hung up. Then an interviewer for the Canadian Broadcasting Corporation called to talk to me. "About what?" I asked. "Well, I guess your anti-Semitism," he said rather weakly.

In the meantime in my church a minister's wife, who had never been near the Middle East and hadn't read much either, wrote a long and what I thought was a rather uninformed letter, which I sent back explaining we had a lot of correspondence waiting to be published and that I had an idea she hadn't read both sides. If I were unfair, and she had, I told her to send the letter back and I'd print it.

Her letter began, "I was ashamed to be a Canadian on that

day that our Canadian forces in the UN in Gaza returned to Canada at the whim of a dictator. . . ." and continued on that level for a few thousand emotional words.

She went to the Zionists and her letter was soon all over the place. It appeared as a full page ad in the *St. Catharines Standard*, purchased by the local synagogue.

Later the author came to me, perturbed at some of the things she was beginning to learn about Zionists. We had a long, friendly talk. But she has continued and her letters keep turning up here and there with the anti-Semitic charge.

An attack came from a young New Testament professor, David Dempson, of my own college, who didn't say anything to me but felt it necessary to write a letter to the local paper, full of innuendo and saying I was "using anti-Semitic sources." I had never seen or heard of the sources he mentioned. He charged that the *Observer* had opposed Jews on such things as religious education in the schools – we were for it and some local rabbis and Unitarians were against it in Canada, although not in Israel! – and a proposed hate literature law. (The latter was vigorously opposed by some of Canada's most distinguished Jewish jurists, but generally the Jewish people supported it.) Dempson seemed to imply: "If you don't want to be thought anti-Semitic, don't disagree with Jewish people on political matters." He wrote later, "Forrest insists he is not anti-Semitic." I hadn't, nor did I think I had to insist.

If I had made an imbalanced attack on Israel it wouldn't have been so bad. But after the attacks began I went back over my materials and concluded that I had really been more unfair to the Palestinians than to the Zionists.

James Peters, a prominent Toronto Arab whom I had never met, wrote a letter defending me against critics in the local press. Later I met him at a party and he said, "I wrote that without having read your pieces. When I did I said, 'With friends like that who needs enemies.' " However, he said he considered my heart was in the right place even though he disagreed with some of my conclusions.

It was apparent that the local Zionists hadn't read me either. One day I had lunch with the editor of the *Canadian Jewish News*. I felt he had been mercilessly unfair but he was a nice and an interesting person. We went to my office afterwards and he casually picked up a copy of the *Observer* from my desk.

"So this is your paper! I've never seen it!" he said.

I almost shouted in amazement. "You've been attacking me for months . . . what do you base it on?"

"Oh, people tell me what you say," he said with a rather disarming grin.

But apparently he hadn't been told I'd said some nice things about Israel and some harsh things about Arabs.

I had been so impressed by the Israeli experts in Jerusalem that I had echoed their prediction (which turned out to be wrong) that Israel would do a better job of looking after the Palestine refugees than the Arabs had done. I wrote:

"Refugees in the notorious Gaza Strip are already better off than under Egypt." And, "Israel is determined, with help from the west, to move towards solution of the refugee problem within her new 'borders' and prove to the world that she can do a better job than the Arabs did."

"The Israeli public is bitter about Syrian intrusions over the past 19 years and is threatened by Jordan radio's advice to returning refugees to be a 'thorn in the side' of Israel."

"Israel invites the leaders of the Christian and Muslim communities to 'dialogue' and hopes to make the holy places of all faiths accessible to all people."

I said a lot of other things that must have made informed Arabs shake their heads about me, and some that would make them nod about their own leaders:

"Israel's public relations are good; Arab PR is bad. The Arab nations have been very unwise in denying visas to North American Jews. Many Jews are conscientious and fair-minded and their judgment has not been distorted by Zionist propaganda."

I wrote:

"Arab spokesmen have been very foolish in talking about throwing Israel into the sea. Much of their propaganda is hate-filled and all the assurances from moderate Arabs that we should not take such threats literally or seriously cannot offset the effusions of extremists from Cairo, Amman and Damascus."

I wrote too:
"Our criticism is not of the way Israel fought the war last June. Many grave charges have been made about Israel's expansionist policies. We interpret her brilliant victory as necessary defensive action taken against continued military threats from Egypt, Syria and Jordan."

That is not the way I see it all now, but that is the way many Israelis, as well as the rest of the world, saw it – unless they had informed themselves at greater depth than most of us had.

However I also said that:
"We condemn the . . . harsh, inhumane treatment of the refugees now and the 19-year old record of inhumanity to the Palestinian refugees. . . . Any policy that denies them the basic right to return to their homes or obstructs, hinders or delays that return is criminal."
I entitled that editorial "Injustice." It got quoted – a lot. And that was what turned the Zionists on.

During all this I began to discover new friends – Jews who had dared to question Israeli policies and suddenly found themselves in worse trouble than I was. The crank stuff on the telephone had got so bad my family insisted I delist. Another A. C. Forrest in the Toronto telephone directory had to delist too.

Among the things I missed, though, were the calls from friendly Jews who said, "Keep it up – you're right but we can't say anything." There were others, sincere pro-Israeli Jews who were convinced I was not only dead wrong but a threat to them and a dangerous menace to decent Christian-

Jewish relations. I had time for sincere persons who disagreed. I didn't have much time for the professionals and the rabbis who know what the score is in the Middle East but tried to pressure me into silence.

There are two things you can do when you get in such a controversy – back away and shut up (and probably resent those who forced you to keep quiet and hate yourself for giving in), or press on. I pressed on. But I found a good number of editors and broadcasters who weren't going to press.

I wrote about my experiences. It was a fairly light-hearted piece. I had become used to the attacks. To my astonishment I began to hear from Americans in places high and low to whom the same had happened. Some had been ruined professionally; some had been terribly hurt. Later, when I went to Beirut to live, I found I was known for the piece I had written about the Zionist criticism and unknown for the many more important things I thought I had done.

Then I began to discover that mine was a normal experience endured by all sorts of non-professional people who dared to say anything about the Middle East that criticized or even implied a criticism of Israel.

William Heine, Editor of the *London (Ontario) Free Press* and an experienced traveller in the Middle East, after doing several series of blunt articles, wrote: "Writers who try to present the Arab view are vociferously condemned privately and in public; every possible kind of pressure is exerted to try to silence the unwelcome opinion, and as a last resort charges of anti-Semitism have been levelled. It makes writers wary – it also makes them mad. The Arabs, incidentally, are the same; anything less than complete agreement is often considered gross criticism and resented vigorously."

One Jewish friend tells me, "It's because you are a clergyman and so many of our people from Europe remember that when some churchman began sounding off they had better be prepared for another pogrom."

I was invited by several Jewish groups to speak to them. In one case it was an on-again, off-again matter over several months until the young lad in a synagogue youth group who asked me admitted they were under a lot of pressure from their

45

parents to withdraw the invitation. The Jewish press was keeping up the attack and I was labelled, "that creature," a "virulent anti-Zionist," and "an enemy of Israel." One Toronto rabbi said I had admitted "I had always hated Israel." One rabbi at a distinguished social gathering told me, "You'll have a page in Jewish history along with Adolph Hitler." He also said loudly, "I'd like to know what the Arabs are paying you."

Finally the synagogue speaking engagement was on, on condition that after I had spoken I would be answered by the Israeli Consul-General in Toronto, Mr. Aba Gefen. I concentrated on "the new refugees," and reported what I saw.

Mr. Gefen embarked on a personal attack. Where had I been when Hitler was coming to power, and where was I when he was killing six million Jews? (When I got a chance, although I don't like that kind of question, I admitted I had been a boy in high school when Hitler came to power and later wore an RCAF uniform during World War II, although I had done all my service in Canada and most of my fighting with Commanding Officers.) Gefen said:

"... these refugees were urged by the Arab governments to return westward and incited to destroy Israel from within. And now thousands of them could be returning under categories approved by the Israeli government, their return is wantonly prevented. Thousands of refugees have Israeli permits to return, but the Jordanian government declared none will return."

That was in November, 1967.

The thoroughly documented fact then was that a hundred and seventy thousand refugees in Jordan filled out forms applying to return (Israel says only a hundred and fifty thousand) and Israel issued permits for twenty thousand to go back. Only fourteen thousand returned. The reasons why the other six thousand permits were not used are many. The main one was that in many cases Israel approved the return of part of a family and said "no" to others, such as boys of seventeen or eighteen. Rather than split up and run the risk of never seeing their children again families decided to stick it out in the refugee camps.

46

I thought then that the Consul was deliberately misleading his audience. I have concluded since that he actually believed what he said. After a time I was honoured by attention from the Anti-Defamation League, which commissioned a Zionist professor named Arnold Ages, who had been in on the attack, to do some real research. He made a study of the *Observer* over some twenty years – a very selective one for a research professor I must add – and the ADL circulated their thirteen page single-spaced document among the newspapers and radio stations of Canada. It ended with a quotation from a line-toeing fundamentalist premillenialist, Dr. Douglas Young of Jerusalem, who had attacked my call for a "peace with justice settlement now."

Young addressed an Open Letter to me which was apparently published in the *Jerusalem Post*. It began "J'Accuse," and continued:

"If war comes to the Middle East again, historians will record that your pen, which could have been a contributory to peace . . . will, like a sword of war, drip with the blood of the wounded and dead on both sides."

That quotation now continues to turn up here and there in Zionist attacks on me; even rabbis with standing quote it, as though Young were an authority. In Jerusalem Dr. Douglas Young and his Institute are almost unknown to the intelligent Christian community.

Somehow I attracted the attention of an American syndicated columnist by the name of Lester Kinsolving – an Episcopal clergyman, I understand. I find time and time again when I am being interviewed somewhere a clipping of one of his columns on me is dragged out and quoted at me.

His column started with the statement that "North America's most outstanding advocate of the Arab cause and critic of Israel is, according to the secretary general of the Arab League . . ." – me! This was based, he proceeds to say, on a statement attributed by a Cairo newspaper to Mr. Abdel Hassouna, the Secretary General of the Arab League, when he was defending the work of the League's information officers around the world. "The only individual he mentioned however was the Rev. A. C. Forrest." So that makes me the outstanding advocate!

In 1968 I met Mr. Hassouna at a Rights of Man Congress in Beirut; he was quite nice. I didn't get the impression he considered me his top man in North America though. In fact, I don't think he remembered having heard of me. But then he probably hadn't read Mr. Kinsolving's column.

One of Kinsolving's greatest tributes was a misquotation about my war record. The columnist said I had said that "In my four years as a prisoner, the Germans never treated me so harshly as the Israelis are treating the Arabs," I was never a prisoner of the Germans. I was never across the Atlantic until 1957, nor did I ever say so. Michael Adams made that statement in an article about conditions in the Gaza. Mr. Kinsolving just seemed to have his clippings all mixed up.

Kinsolving attributed a number of statements to Dr. Robert McClure, the Moderator of The United Church of Canada. One of the statements attributed to him, defending my work, sounded fine. Some of the others were rather startling. The Moderator told Kinsolving, Kinsolving claimed, that he was in favour of a settlement in which Israel would "retain all of the Golan Heights, the West Bank, Jerusalem and Sinai from a boundary running 40 miles east of Suez." It didn't sound like Dr. McClure. I must say I didn't take Mr. Kinsolving very seriously at the time, but the more this got quoted at me the more I wondered how far wrong he was in the things I didn't know about. One day I discovered in my files one of the numerous clippings from one of the numerous papers which had been sent to me, and sent it to Dr. McClure with a query, "Did you say that?" Dr. McClure ran a pencil around the worst quotes and wrote "no" and sent it back.

The Kinsolving piece is illustrative of the irresponsibility of some churchmen and some of the church press on this issue. The evidence is that this is the most pressing international issue of our time. Informed churchmen have a feeling of desperation sometimes, a conviction that the mass media are more harmful than helpful. I have come to the conclusion through my own experiences that we can't expect much intelligent discussion of this subject from the editors, publishers, and broadcasters, nor from the universities. I have been appalled by the numbers of persons who do know, and could help, but feel they have to beg off because of the sensitive positions they hold. This makes it more important that the church press does a thorough job.

I have often been asked if I have been pressured by my church to shut up or get out. It's not that kind of church. In fact I don't know any church that would be that kind – although I know of a few individuals within the church who are. The pastor in his pulpit and the editor of a church paper are still the freest men in the world when it comes to saying forthrightly what they believe to be true.

As I wrote the above another clipping dropped on my desk, from the *Intermountain Jewish News*, which introduces a few columns of comment about anti-Semitism with:

"The Rev. A. C. Forrest, editor of The United Church Observer, an anti-Israel publication, has turned the official organ of The United Church of Canada into his own vituperative war machine against Israel. . . ."

It was another mark of a calculated, sustained attempt to discredit me and destroy any influence I might have in the Christian community. The technique of the outright lie, the innuendo, the smear, the pressures on my friends, on editors who have published my stuff, have been a bitter revelation to me.

I have been forced reluctantly to the conclusion that there are a lot of gutless editors and publishers and public officials about. The future will show tragically, I fear, that the price paid for bending to these pressures and avoiding unpleasant controversy has been costly.

During all this I have discovered that the most enlightened and penetrating comment on the Middle East has been written and spoken by Jewish intellectuals. The irritation I have experienced is trivial compared to the persecution some of them have suffered at the hands of their own people. My admiration for the courageous Jew who reports what he believes to be true about Israel and the Arabs is without limits.

nine

The Palestine Problem

I CHATTED ONE NIGHT FOR A LONG TIME WITH AN ATTRACTIVE Israeli girl in Nazareth.

I told her I admired her and the other young Israelis I met, and why. But I added that she was just like young Arabs I had met at the universities in Beirut and Jordan. "Except for one thing – you don't hate them, but they hate you. And the reason is they were away from home during the June war of 1967 and Israel won't let them back. They have lost everything."

She was sympathetic. "I know in war sad things happen and innocent people are hurt." Then she added, "Do you know what I would do if I were they? I would join Fateh."

She went on to tell me how she felt about Israel. "My people have been persecuted down the centuries all over the earth. We couldn't trust anyone. Now we have our own land – maybe you don't like the way we got it, but we have got it and we are going to keep it. For we learned we can't trust anybody, not you, or the Americans, or the British!" And with an angry flourish she added, "and don't tell me the United Nations. To hell with the United Nations."

In Jordan and Beirut and Cario I heard much the same. Young Palestinians will scoff at what they call "the reactionary Arab states," they are fed up with the UN and with the US and "the West" and they don't trust Russia or China either. "We Palestinians have made up our minds. We will have to do it ourselves."

The struggle cannot be reduced to these simple terms. But

it's in the suffering of decent people you see the tragedy of it all. I suppose no one from outside can take the dimensions or measure the depth of the tragedy in the Middle East. It is easy to become confused or lost in the complexities. It is difficult to remain uninvolved.

I could not remain detached or uninvolved. Take the woman at the bridge with her four children, saying goodbye to her husband. It is so unnecessary; yet things like that happen every day at the bridge. And those people can do nothing about it except hate. And somehow hating, with all its destructiveness, gives some dignity and strength to those who hate. They are hating hard in the Middle East today.

The quarrel is over the possession of that strip of land that stretches from Dan to Beersheba, between the Jordan River and the Mediterranean Sea. The trouble began between a remnant of Jewish people, who organized a Return to the land their fathers once possessed for a short time three thousand years ago, and the residents of Palestine whose fathers have lived there for many centuries.

Palestine has come to be known among western Christians as "The Holy Land." Its geography is more familiar to those reared in Protestant Sunday Schools than that of any other land save their own. Its towns and cities, the Jordan River, Galilee, and the Dead Sea have become sacred because of their association with the Bible and the life of Jesus.

But Palestine has never been a land of peace. Its location as the meeting place for Asia, Africa, and Europe is too strategic, militarily, politically, and economically, for the world to leave it alone. Through it the ancient caravans travelled. On Mount Megiddo, presiding over the rich plains of Esdraelon, the horses of King Solomon were stabled. It was a saying among ancient conquerors that he who held Megiddo could hold back all invaders, and the prophets predicted that the world's last great battle would be fought there.

The "troubles" had their beginnings in the dream of Zionist Jews for a land of their own. No people needed a land more than the Jewish people did. The Jews were expelled from Jerusalem by the Romans in 135 AD and scattered over the world. A few trickled back and small Jewish communities persisted in Galilee and surrounding parts of Palestine. Jewish volunteers joined the Persian invasion, when Jerusalem was captured in 615 and held for eight years. Twice during the centuries short-lived Jewish States were established outside of Palestine. Early in the sixth century a core of Jews ruled by Arab converts established a state in Yemen and between the 8th and 10th centuries another Jewish state comprising converted Khazars was established on the lower Volga.

Somehow – it seems to have been miraculous – the Jews survived as a people. They were faithful to the Law, their Scriptures, and to the old and complicated rituals. During times of persecution, especially, they dreamed that some day they might return to Jerusalem and the glories of their past.

Several attempts were made to establish settlements in Palestine during the 19th century. In 1837 Sir Moses Montefiore, a very wealthy Jewish broker from London, returned from Palestine enthusiastic about the possibilities of Jewish settlement. He had found communities of Jewish people, totalling about eight thousand in Jerusalem, Hebron, Tiberias, and Safad. He enthused over the olive groves, the vineyards, the pasture lands, the figs, walnuts, almonds, and mulberries, and the fine fields of wheat, barley, and lentils. "It is land that could produce almost anything in abundance with very little skill and very little labour," he said, convinced that Jews would find success more easily there than by emigrating elsewhere.

Sir Moses had limited success with his plans but others followed and a few Jewish settlements and kibbutzim were established. In Russia, student groups formed clubs to organize emigration to Palestine.

In the 1880's in Vienna, Theodor Hertzl, an assimilated and secular Jew, was deeply distressed over the situation of his people. He first proposed they be officially converted to Christianity and suggested seeing the Pope to that end. Dissuaded from that, he came up with a new idea – the mass migration of Jews to a land where they would have supremacy. He opposed suggestions of "infiltration" on the assumption that as soon as a native population was threatened immigration of Jews would be stopped.

52

Those who supported him were convinced that Palestine was the place to go. The myth developed that Palestine was uninhabited. Actually, there were over five hundred thousand people in Palestine.

A proposal to hold a conference of Zionists in Munich, Germany, was dropped because of the opposition of the German rabbis. They said that "attempts to found a Jewish national state in Palestine were contrary to the Messianic promises of Judaism."

The first congress of Zionists was held in Basle, Switzerland, in 1897. They approved of the establishment of a home for the Jewish people in Palestine.

The idea of a "home" rather than a "state" persisted in Zionist thought for many years. The Tenth congress, held at Basle in 1911, was opened by the president with these words:

"Only those suffering from gross ignorance, or actuated by malice, could accuse us of the desire of establishing an independent Jewish Kingdom. . . . Not a Jewish state but a home in the ancient land of our forefathers. . . ."

The years from 1897 to 1917 were full of vigorous efforts to recruit immigrants for Palestine, to raise funds, and to secure political support.

Palestinian Arabs were not troubled. They had always known Jews and got along with them well. The immigrants brought money and bought land. Even when the famous Balfour Declaration was made in 1917 there was no undue alarm, except among those who noted that Great Britain had made inconsistent promises – to the Arabs that they could have their independence, and to the Jews that they could have a National Home in Palestine.

Later it was learned that the British had agreed with the French to divide Palestine, the Lebanon, and Syria – at that time all one country, really, under the Turks – between them.

The Balfour Declaration said:

"His Majesty's Government view with favour the establishment in Palestine of a national home for the Jewish people, and will use their best efforts to facilitate the achievement of this object, it being clearly understood that nothing shall be done which may prejudice the civil and religious rights of existing non-Jewish communities in Palestine or the rights and political status enjoyed by Jews in any other country."

Millions of copies of the declaration were scattered throughout the Jewish world, but it was not mentioned officially in Palestine for several years.

The object was not a State but a Home for the Jews. The rights of the Palestinians would be safe-guarded. And in order to protect Jews in other lands from too strenuous recruiting – or from a possible reaction, "You've got a home of your own now, so you can leave here . . ." from anti-Semitic politicians – Jewish rights abroad were to be protected too.

By 1918 Palestine had a population of about seven hundred thousand, of whom six hundred and forty-four thousand were Arabs and fifty-six thousand Jews according to Professor Constantine Zureik of the American University of Beirut. The eight per cent Jewish minority owned two per cent of the land.

Following World War I and the setting up of the British Mandate, Jewish immigration was stepped up and the Palestinian Arabs began their active protest.

I must skim over the various developments but pause to note the statement of British Policy by Winston Churchill, the Colonial Secretary, of June 1922. Churchill emphasized that Palestine was not to become a Jewish National Home, but that "such a home should be founded *in Palestine*." He pointed out that "all citizens of Palestine . . . shall be Palestinian. . . ." He added, "It is not the imposition of a Jewish nationality upon the inhabitants of Palestine as a whole, but the further development of the existing community, with the assistance of Jews in other parts of the world, in order that it may become a centre in which the Jewish people as a whole may take, on grounds of religion and race, an interest and pride."

The Palestine population soon became alarmed by the stepped-up immigration of European Jews. During the following years the Jews organized militarily to enforce their

54

immigration and settlement and Arabs resisted ineffectively. Several commissions were sent to investigate, and reported that the problems in Palestine resulted from the fear of the Arabs that they would be dispossessed by the mass immigration of Zionists.

During the thirties persecution of Jews was increased in Germany and this was climaxed by Hitler's murder of millions; and following the war the Jewish remnant was in desperate need of a place to go.

Britain had announced her intention to withdraw from the Mandate and the UN decided in November 1947, to partition Palestine between the Arabs and Jews. Britain withdrew in the midst of fierce fighting in May 1948, and the Jewish community declared the founding of the State of Israel. It was recognized immediately by many major nations. Hundreds of thousands of Arabs fled as Arab armies marched against Israel and were soundly beaten.

Since then the Palestine problem has taken on a new dimension. Professor Constantine Zureik, speaking to a conference of World Christians in Beirut in May 1970, summed it up:

"By 1946 as a result of the Balfour declaration and its implementation by Great Britain and Mandatory Power, the Jewish population had risen almost 11 times to 608,000, and the Arabs to 1,283,000. The Jewish property did not exceed 5.66 per cent of the area.

"In 1947 the UN decided to partition Palestine. The Jewish state was to cover 14,500 sq. km. while the Arab state did not exceed 11,000. The Jews who had less than 6 per cent of land of the total were given 56 per cent of it, including most of the fertile parts. The proposed Jewish state was to contain 509,000 Arabs, and 499,000 Jews. The bulk of the Jewish population had been admitted during the mandate and less than one third had acquired Palestinian citizenship. Between the UN decision of November 20th, 1947 and the actual close of the Mandate and withdrawal on May 15th, 1948, Jewish regular and irregular forces seized most of the Arab cities of Palestine and scores of Arab villages. They not only forcefully overran territory lying within the proposed Jewish state . . . but also cities and scores of localities assigned to the Arab states including Jaffa and Acre as well as the new City of Jerusalem. This process continued through the Arab-Israeli war with the result . . . the total area which fell under Israeli control rose to almost 80 per cent of the country."

About seven hundred and thirty thousand Palestinians were made homeless. The Israeli immigrants took over their lands, businesses, and houses, paying no compensation.

The UN tried. The United Nations Relief and Works Agency was set up to feed, provide schools and medical help for the refugees and to shelter them. Cease-fire and armistice agreements were worked out and an expeditionary force was sent to help preserve the peace. The armistice arrangements were to be supervised.

But all through the years there was no peace. The UN said the refugees who were ready to return and live at peace should be allowed to go back or be compensated. There were some half-hearted, limited offers unacceptable to the defeated. In 1956 Israel attacked and took the Gaza Strip and Sinai, but was condemned by the UN and forced by President Eisenhower to withdraw.

In 1967, during the June "six-day war," Israel took the Gaza Strip, Sinai, all of Palestine, and part of Syria. Professor Zureik adds:

"The result of all this is that a people, the Palestinian Arabs, has been deprived of its homeland and has become totally homeless or under occupation."

There had been "a Jewish problem" in the world for over two thousand years: the Jews were unjustly treated again and again. In an attempt to solve that problem a new one has been created – the Palestinian problem.

Some Israeli Jews say that Palestinians are not a separate nation – just Arabs and the Arabs have lots of land and many countries. Why shouldn't the Palestinians just go away and disappear among their brothers?

But the Palestinians reply,

"Now we are a people too. We're not Kuwaiti's or Syrians, we are Palestinians. Palestine is our country because we inherited it, tilled the fields, and built our homes. We want it back. The Zionists claim Palestine is theirs because God gave it to their fathers. They have not lived there for nineteen hundred years. Some of us were driven out in 1948, and others of us in 1967. We believe it is our right to return and we intend to go back."

So the struggle goes on. The homeless have tripled in number and the territory occupied by Israel has been increased many times. Three wars have been fought and skirmishing continues. The whole Middle East dangles on the edge of war.

ten

Myths about
the Middle East

WHEN A TYPICAL NORTH AMERICAN GOES TO LIVE IN THE
Middle East, he suffers from what is called "cultural shock."
Abroad, he is likely to be shattered by the discovery of his
own ignorance; back home, he is dismayed by the misconceptions of his friends.

"I hate to admit how ignorant I was," Canadian broadcaster
James Reed told me after a few days in the Middle East. "Before I arrived, I thought that the Arabs were poor and backward, that they were all Moslems, and that the commandos
were a bunch of wild-eyed terrorists. Those myths have been
exploded fast."

Those are but three of the myths about the Israeli-Arab
world generally accepted as facts of life in the United States
and Canada.They are much less likely to be believed in a
better-informed Europe.

A person doesn't have to go to live in the Middle East or
even take a trip abroad – although in my opinion nothing helps
us understand our reading better than a visit to the Middle
East to both sides. A careful study of a few selected books,
preferably books written by international observers who have
spent some time working on both sides in the Middle East,
plus some of the basic UN documents, will prove a shock to
most persons too.

Obviously there is some truth – distorted though it may be
– behind all these beliefs. We have, I sincerely believe, a res-

ponsibility to strip away the propaganda, to understand and interpret the myths and to let the truth come through.

Here are fifteen myths:

1. *"Israel is a poor little nation surrounded by hostile Arabs."*

This myth was exploded by the revelations that followed the June 1967 war. Gentiles discovered that when fighting for Israel the Israeli Jews are superb soldiers in a mighty military machine.

"There are fewer than three million Jews in Israel. They are surrounded by sixty to one hundred million Arabs depending on how you study the map. And the Arabs are increasingly hostile," the myth continues. But remember "little Japan," or that tight "little island" called Britain in the nineteenth century, or centuries of Middle Eastern history: it is not the size of the country but the size of the army, and not the number of soldiers but the quality of equipment and training that count. And Israel is backed up by an enormously efficient international organization.

Even as far back as 1948, as British General and Middle East expert Glubb Pasha points out, Israel had sixty-five thousand troops ready for combat; the Arabs had twenty-one and a half thousand. Right now few have any doubt that Israel could take Amman, Damascus, and Beirut tomorrow, or at least within the week, as far as military might is concerned.

2. *"The Arabs are poor and backward."*

There is just enough truth in this, just enough evidence, to persuade the superficial observer that it is completely true. One could say somewhat the same thing of North America after viewing a Communist propaganda film about Alabama or a well-chosen American slum.

I could write about the great cities, the splendid universities, the culture, the science, the people, my Arab friends and their children who speak four languages, and the several countries where there is free education from nursery school to Ph.D.

Let me just say that if you believe this myth you will be startled after a trip to the Middle East, and you will be angered by the way you were misled by so much in the North American press.

3. *"The Arabs are all Moslems."*

Most Arabs are. But approximately half of Lebanon is Christian. In addition, there are six million Coptic Orthodox Christians in the United Arab Republic. About one-tenth of Palestine was Christian. Syria is about one-tenth Christian.

While there are tensions between Christians and Moslems there is remarkable understanding too. And if anyone thinks that the growing bitterness of the Middle East is only between Moslem and Jew, he is very wrong. Christians who live in the Arab countries and in Occupied Territory share the deep sense of injustice the Arab Moslem feels over being dispossessed from his Palestinian home. A large number of these dispossessed Arabs are Christians themselves!

4. *"The Israelis want peace and Arabs want war."*

I have spent enough time in Israel and in Arab countries to believe that the common people of all countries want peace.

Officially, the Arab governments most concerned have accepted the November 22, 1967, UN resolution and declare their willingness to implement it. One condition as laid down by the United Nations is for Israel to withdraw from the territories she occupied during the June war. Another is a just settlement of the refugee problem. But Israel has been digging in steadily and settling down fast. She has annexed East Jerusalem contrary to United Nations instructions. She has refused to let the new crop of refugees return to their camps on the West bank against the unanimous (except for Israel) vote of the UN.

Israel says loudly that she wants a peace settlement. But in her actions she makes every Arab think she is aggressive and expansionist. Israel insists on dealing directly with individual Arab states; the Arabs want to negotiate through the United Nations. But no state represents the conquered Palestinians and they are the big losers in this situation. They themselves insist that Cairo, Amman, and Beirut cannot represent them.

60

Then there is the Zionist record of terrorism in Palestine! The Zionists set out to conquer Palestine by immigration. The amazingly successful combination of pressure on governments abroad, fund-raising, skilfully organized underground immigration, and a sustained programme of propaganda, would not have achieved their goal without the activities of terrorists working skilfully with the Jewish army against both the British and Palestinians.

The UN partition plan gave the Jewish-Zionists fifty-four per cent of the land. During the 1948 war they increased this substantially and now they have it all, plus big hunks of Jordanian, Syrian, and UAR territory.

The one-time Arab majority lost their lands. Some now live within Israel as second class citizens while Jews immigrate from any part of the world to have first-class citizenship when or even before they arrive in Israel. Other Arabs, residing in Occupied Territory as conquered people, live in fear of being arrested by Israeli authorities or of seeing their homes and property destroyed. Still others are virtually homeless and exist in the tented camps of Jordan or beyond.

The Arabs say that this is unjust. They want peace, but they also want these wrongs corrected. Israel wants peace, but, apparently, on a conqueror's terms. Most Arabs believe – rightly or wrongly – that Israel wishes to expand further. Lebanon is particularly fearful of losing the southern part of her land. The Resistance movement now is convinced that Israel's agression and racism can only be stopped through armed conflict.

5. *"The Arab fedayeen or commandos are terrorists."*

Some are. There are more than a dozen groups, now organized under one central command, but some still act quite independently. Some, such as Fateh, eschew acts of terrorism and make their attacks only on military objectives. Others, having learned from the Stern gang and other Jewish terrorist groups who drove their fathers out of Palestine, have adopted the same methods.

However, the vast majority of the Arab people look upon the fedayeen as "our boys," freedom fighters struggling to regain their homes, the military arm of a Resistance movement aimed at turning Palestine into a free democratic state where Christian, Jew, and Moslem may live peacefully together with each man having a vote.

6. *"The refugees could have stayed but they ran away on the advice of Arab governments."*

This falsehood has been denied so often by many authoritative persons. Let me quote one of the most recent statements — one made by the distinguished John Davis, who probably knows more about Arab refugees than any other American. He was Commissioner-General of UNRWA and has recently written *The Evasive Peace*. He says, "The extent to which the refugees were savagely driven out by the Israelis as a deliberate master-plan has been insufficiently recognized."

7. *"The Arab countries have done nothing for their own refugees."*

I think I will let Dr. John Davis answer that one too. He wrote:
"The evidence is quite to the contrary. The refugee host countries of Jordan, UAR, Syria, and Lebanon have been generous and hospitable to the refugees. In direct assistance they have spent more than $100 million, mostly for education, health services, campsites, housing, road improvement, and the maintenance of security on refugee camps. . . . The people of those countries have borne with courage the economic, social, and other sacrifices and other hardships resulting from the presence of large numbers of refugees within their borders. Contrary to much western thinking, the Arab host governments have also helped qualified young refugees obtain employment both within the host countries and elsewhere."

8. *"The refugees could be easily accommodated in other Arab countries but they are kept in UNRWA camps for propaganda purposes."*

62

Sixty per cent are not, nor have they ever been in camps.

But, as John Davis points out:

"Following the upheaval of 1948, virtually all able bodied male refugees who possessed skills . . . found jobs almost immediately and became self-supporting. In contrast the farmers . . . comprising 70 per cent . . . did not fare so well. The problem is . . . that the refugees have become surplus farm workers in an era when the world and the Arab countries particularly has a surplus of farm laborers . . . hence the rural refugee from Palestine became dependent upon international charity. . . . The reasons are not that they were held hostages . . . but they were unemployable."

In addition, the Palestinians don't want to be settled in Libya or Egypt or Iraq or Kuwait. Thousands of them are working in other Arab places but many keep their families near the old borders, for their dearest wish is to go back.

9. *"Israel could not absorb the refugees. It would be national suicide."*

General Dayan commented on this once. "Economically we can [let them return] but I think it is not in accord with our national aims for the future. It would turn Israel into a bi-national or poly-national state instead of a Jewish state, and we want a Jewish state." This protest has always amused me. Up until 1967 Israel always used the excuse that for security reasons she could not risk having any of the dangerous refugees within her frontiers. When she occupied the West Bank and Gaza, although she worked hard to drive out and keep out as many as possible, she accepted with considerable enthusiasm the "new territories" even though they contained over half a million Arabs.

10. *"While Arabs resort to terrorism Israel does not commit atrocities."*

Let's take just one report by the Red Cross, commented on by Davis. "Deir Yassin, an Arab village to the east of Jerusalem, was attacked on April 9, 1948, by two terrorist groups, the

63

Irgun Zvai Leumi and the Stern Gang. According to the eye-witness account of the International Red Cross representative 254 men, women, and children were slaughtered and many of their bodies were stuffed into a well. . . . The Red Cross reporting on the butchery said it had all the marks of deliberate massacre by a band admirably disciplined and acting under orders. . . ."

11. *"The refugees are better off under Israel than when they were under Arabs."*

Some on the West Bank may be. Many are far worse off – in Gaza for example. On some parts of the West Bank, too, conditions have deteriorated badly. And they live under a constant threat, they feel, of having their homes blown up or their villages destroyed. Even those who may be better off financially resent being "occupied" and are fearful of Israel's intent to Judaize the "new territories."

12. *"The Israelis have made the desert bloom; the Arabs have neglected their land."*

Far be it for me to take anything away from those industrious and decent Israeli settlers who drained the swamps, irrigated the desert, and planted the trees. They work hard. They are efficient.

And Arab lands are undeveloped. But when I first visited Egypt's Liberation Province in the Nile Delta, I discovered that the UAR in that one development had reclaimed almost the precise acreage, without publicity, that Israel has reclaimed in Palestine. There is an untold story of vast projects of reclamation, irrigation, and development from the Russian-financed Aswan Dam to church-sponsored agricultural and reforestation developments in the valleys of upper Jordan.

Many of those orchards pointed out by Israeli guides to wide-eyed tourists are more than twenty years old. They were planted by Arabs during the British mandate. The Israelis confiscated them.

64

Israelis are justly proud of their achievements in the lovely city of Haifa. Nevertheless, Haifa was a fine city before Israel was born.

We should not ignore the backwardness – by western standards – of much of the Arab world. But we should not forget either that the Arabs, rather than being allowed to progress, have instead been conquered, ruled, and exploited by others for centuries.

13. *"Israel is a bastion of western democracy in an undemocratic world."*

There is much to admire about democracy in Israel, such as vigorous criticism of Israeli policies in the Knesset, private discussion, and the press. Those western Zionists, who label any critic of Israel as anti-Semitic, could learn much from this criticism.

But to the Arab and to every objective foreigner I know who has worked and traveled in both Israel and the Arab countries, Israel is a western imperialist, expansionist, military power. How can there be true democracy and freedom in a country which says, "We want to be Jewish" – and treats its non-Jewish minority as inferiors?

The most penetrating comments on this are being made by Jewish prophets within and outside Israel. I. F. Stone, in the *New York Review of Books*, quotes former Israeli Prime Minister David Ben Gurion. Mr. Ben Gurion said, "Israel is the country of the Jews and only of the Jews. Every Arab who lives here has the same right as any minority citizen in any country of the world, but he must admit the fact that he lives in a Jewish country." Stone adds, "The implication must chill Jews in the outside world."

Stone continues, "Israel is creating a kind of moral schizophrenia in world Jewry. In the outside world the welfare of Jewry depends on the maintenance of secular, nonracial, pluralistic societies. In Israel, Jewry finds itself defending a society in which mixed marriages cannot be legalized, in which non-Jews have a lesser status than Jews, and in which the ideal is racial and exclusionist. Jews must fight elsewhere for their very security and existence against principles and practices they find themselves defending in Israel."

Or, to cite another great Jewish prophet, the measure of whose greatness may be estimated by the vigour of Zionist attacks against him, Rabbi Elmer Berger:

"In Israel there are laws seeking to bind Jews of all countries into an obligatory nationalist relationship with this new state. At the same time there are laws which discriminate against more than a million and a half 'Palestine refugees' who are recognized by the world to have legitimate claims to citizenship rights in the territories now comprising or occupied by Israel. There are discriminatory practices against the more than half of Israel's Jews who are Arab or Orientals. There are laws which prevent the full and equal practice of any Judaism in this 'Jewish' state other than the interpretation of Judaism vested in the recognized religious-political parties."

In the language of Henry A. Byroade of the American State Department, Israel has adopted "the attitude of conqueror and the conviction that force and a policy of retaliatory killings is the only policy that their neighbours will understand."

14. *"The Arabs are against the Jews."*

The Arabs are emphatic about this. I must have heard a thousand times, "We are not against Jews. We are against Zionists."

The fear is that as generations who do not know Jews personally grow up in the camps of Jordan the distinction will disappear. There is some anti-Semitism in the Middle East. It is likely to increase if a solution is not found and if Israel continues to pursue her present policies, encouraged by the uncritical support of Jewish Zionists abroad.

15. *"The Arabs want to throw Israel into the sea."*

This has been said often enough and no doubt some Arabs would like to throw some Israelis into the sea or worse. It is this awful threat and fear that disturbs Christians and Jews

66

and responsible Arabs. But it is repudiated by all responsible Arabs, who deeply regret that the threat has been made.

In 1969 I asked Dr. M. H. El Zayyat, then President Nasser's chief spokesman in Cairo, about this statement. He said, "To bear a child out of wedlock is a sin. To destroy the child after it is born is sinful too." The responsible Arab powers want to settle with Israel, have secure boundaries, and end the state of belligerence. But some, such as the UAR, do not want to recognize her in the sense of having formal or trade relations with her. They feel that if there could be an end to belligerency and Israel would stop threatening to expand, if the refugees could be compensated or have their homes back, eventually things could work out. Others, unwilling to have such a settlement, insist that Israel as a Zionist state must be changed or de-Zionized.

There are irresponsible, angry Arabs suffering a deep sense of injustice. There are also irresponsible, threatened Israelis.

eleven

A Kindergarten Lesson
on Islam

IT IS NOT ONLY DIFFICULT, IT IS IMPOSSIBLE TO UNDERSTAND
the Middle East without some knowledge of Islam. More than
eighty per cent of the people are Moslems; there are few un-
believers. Many are devout. Those of us brought up in the West
tend to judge too much by what we were taught in school about
the Crusades. Much of our teaching is as over-simplified and
distorted as it would be if Moslems illustrated their lectures on
Christianity by stories from the Spanish Inquisition.

At a horrible risk of doing a disservice to Islam I am going
to try to pass on some notes on a lecture from a Moslem scholar given to Christians at the Community Church in Beirut in
1969.

Here are some simple facts about Islam he gave us.

First, God is. He is *The* Supreme Being. He is all-powerful,
all-knowing, benevolent, and unique. He will guide his children to serve, to obey, and to worship him.

Secondly, for the Moslem, *the supreme guide* to right living
is the Koran – the Moslem's Bible. Among Moslems there are
fundamentalists and modernists too, and they have their sects
and divisions and denominations; they are as confusing to
Christians as Christian divisions are confusing to Moslems.

Thirdly, Mohammed is God's prophet. He is not the only
prophet, but he is *the* prophet. Our Old Testament prophets
and Jesus are revered too. This means that the good Moslem
has great respect for the Bible and for sincere Jews and Christians. Our teacher told us that "Mohammed for the purposes
of the Koran was a tape-recorder for the Voice of God," just

as for some Christians the Bible is, from cover to cover, the literally inspired Word of God.

Then there are the five pillars of conduct for the Moslem.

First, the bearing of witness: to declare in the presence of two witnesses, "God is, and God is the only Being worthy of the worship of man, and Mohammed is his prophet;" to confess that from the mind and heart with the mouth — and of course then to live that way — is what makes a man a Moslem.

The second pillar is prayer. There are obligatory prayers and optional prayers. But a good Moslem sincerely tries to pray five times a day; immediately after dawn, at noon, during the afternoon, at sunset, and between sunset and midnight. Such prayers are personal. Then on Friday he joins with the neighbourhood at the mosque, and once a year he joins with the whole community or city. Once in a lifetime he makes a pilgrimage to Mecca, to join symbolically with the whole world in prayer.

The third pillar is charity, or almsgiving. This is not a tithe from income but a gift of a fortieth of one's capital. Its major element is what we sometimes call "the need of the giver to give." It has social and personal aspects but the chief is, "it is good for me to give to others. The other thirty-nine parts of my wealth are made sacred when I bestow one-fortieth to feed the poor."

The fourth is fasting from food, drink, tobacco, etc. during Ramadan. For one month a year the good Moslem fasts from dawn to sunset.

The fifth is the pilgrimage to Mecca — but it must not be made if one's journey causes financial embarrassment to one's dependents.

Underneath all of this is the Koran's teaching that a good Moslem does what he can. If he can't pray five times a day, then three times, or twice, or once if he can, and so on.

I must repeat — there is so much left out. It is like a Moslem summing up the Christian religion in a similar space. Our libraries have good books for those who would pursue the subject and I wish more would. But for me the most helpful lesson on Islam is to know good Moslems. Much of what is good in the Palestinian is a product of this faith.

twelve

What Is Zionism?

POLITICAL ZIONISM IS A PHILOSOPHY WHICH SAYS THAT ALL Jews belong to one nation. They need a state of their own to secure their identity, to protect themselves from future outbursts of anti-Semitism, and to develop their culture and civilization. Israel is that state and it is the duty of all Jews to support Israel and, if possible, to go to live in Israel.

There are Zionists and Zionists, even as there are Jews and Jews and Christians and Christians. Dr. Nahum Goldmann, once head of the World Zionist Organization and later head of the World Jewish Congress, says simply:

"I was always a political Zionist in the sense that I believed that Jews must have a state of their own to secure their identity and civilization."

In the beginning Zionists favoured the establishment of a national home of their own in Palestine, but a number of other places such as Uganda, were very seriously considered.

Uri Avnery says the fundamental tenets of Zionism are:

"All Jews of the world are one nation. Israel is a Jewish state created by the Jews and for the Jews all over the world. The Jewish dispersal is a temporary situation and sooner or later all Jews will have to go to Israel, driven if by nothing else inevitable anti-Semitic persecution. The ingathering of the exiles is the raison d'etre of Israel."

70

The Basle Congress in 1897 outlined the Zionist objectives as follows:

"The object of Zionism is the establishment for the Jewish people of a home in Palestine secured by public law." The steps to be taken were:

1. The promotion, on suitable lines, of the colonization of Palestine by Jewish agricultural and industrial workers.
2. The organization and binding together of the whole of Jewry by means of appropriate institutions, local and international, in accordance with the laws of each country.
3. The strengthening and fostering of Jewish national sentiment and consciousness.
4. Preparatory steps towards obtaining Government consent where necessary, to the attainment of the aim of Zionism.

There are of course many Jews who are critical of Zionism and fearful of it. They charge that the Zionists in their zeal to win support and immigrants for Israel will actually stimulate and promote anti-Semitism. Early Zionism was largely a product of anti-Semitism, and one of their fundamental theories was that anti-Semitism is a peculiar disease which has infected or can infect all, or almost all, non-Jews in any country. The mere presence of Jews among Christians is an irritant which generates anti-Semitism, for which there can be no remedy. Therefore, the only way to solve this problem – the most important problem of the Jewish people throughout their history – is for Jews to leave the country of their residence and establish their own state in their historic homeland of Palestine.

Political Zionism was one of two Jewish movements which came into organizational being in 1897. The other was the Socialist Bund. Zionism was a nationalistic movement of the middle class in Eastern Europe. The Bund came out of the poorer and working classes and reflected a very different ideology, for it was based on the very opposite concept – that anti-Semitism, which was real enough at that time, was not a mysterious or perennial evil. "Anti-Semitism has its cause in the economic, political and psychological conditions of society and, like any other human evil, it can be cured by changing the conditions which brought it about. Accordingly the Bund maintains that the Jewish problem is part of the general problem of mankind and can be solved only by the improvement of the lot of humanity as a whole, not by any special panaceas for Jews.

"Instead of an exodus therefore, the Bund advocates greater cooperation with the non-Jewish world, especially with other underprivileged and suffering peoples. Instead of fear and suspicion of non-Jews inculcated by Zionism, the Bund offers faith in mankind and in the brotherhood of all men. Instead of nationalistic justice, which is often oblivious to the suffering of those outside a particular group, the Bund teaches international justice, which combines justified Jewish claims with respect for the rights of other peoples.

"Contrary to the Zionist tenet that Jews are everywhere strangers, the Bund believes that Jews, although they are of a different and distinct national origin are – or should be – equal citizens of their countries, and that they should unite with all other citizens in the common struggle for the victory of labor, democracy and Socialism."

A study of this phrasing gives the key to why young Jews of the New Left, and left-leaning Jews, whether in the labour movement or in academic circles, tend to be critical of Zionism.

The reader may be under the impression that Zionism was a religious movement and may wonder at the secularism of so many leaders in Israel. Note this from the Introduction of *The Middle East Problem*, Geneva 1969:

"As a national movement rooted in secular messianism, Zionism sought not the resolution of the relation between the people of Israel and the God of Israel as in the traditional faith, but between Israel and the nations."

The writer goes on to point out that Theodor Herzl and others sought a charter from the Turkish Sultan and agreements with rulers in the lands where Jews lived. For, while anti-Semitism was the Jewish problem which Zionism sought to solve, it was also a problem for rulers of countries with large numbers of Jews. As Erik Ben Schacter wrote in the same volume, this set the tone for a policy of cooperation between the Zionist movement and the forces of reaction and imperialism.

This is another reason why the North American will often find the wealthy Jews of the community are pro-Zionist and the working Jews are not, and why such states as the USA are solidly behind Israel and the socialist states are not.

In Israel today – and I suppose in the outside world too – there are several significant developments in Zionism, including the rejection of it by former enthusiasts.

There is the gentle, civilized sort of Kibbutz Zionist, such as Simha Flapan, who urges a flexible policy in Israel and a rapprochement to the Arabs: a withdrawal from the occupied territories, an end to the demand for direct negotiations, and a settlement on the basis of the November 22nd resolution of the Security Council. In Dr. Nahum Goldmann you have something of the same spirit. He remembers that the two great challenges to Jews which accounted for the miracle of Israel were "The permanent persecution . . . and the tremendous power of the Jewish religion." Then he goes on to say – as the Bund would have predicted – "These motivations have lost their impact. . . . Anti-Semitism is no more what it used to be in past centuries; Jews everywhere enjoy equality of rights and have become more and more integrated. . . . Jewish religion has ceased to be, at least for the larger part of the Jewish people the great authoritative force which guides their daily life and guarantees their identity and distinctive character. . . ." He says Israel must become a centre of attraction, the greatest challenge for the best, most idealistic elements of the young generation. . . . "An Israel at war cannot become this centre." Goldmann advocates that, "Israel become neutralized. . . . cease to rely on its political and military strength and seek acceptance and guarantee from all the people of the world, under the permanent protection of mankind. . . ."

You have the former Zionists, Uri Avnery and his young followers, who urge that Israel de-Zionize and become in a sense just another state. Avnery claims that young Israeli sabras, who are militantly nationalistic, laugh at the tenets of Zionism. They don't expect, don't want, or don't need "all the Jews of the world to come to Israel." And of course all realistic Israelis know that they are not coming, and that if they continue to keep the gates open for instant Israeli citizenship Israel must remain under constant mobilization, for such threatens further aggression and expansion at the expense of the Arabs.

Then there are the Zionist revisionists, represented by the extreme right wing Herut movement "for peace by annexation of the occupied territories." In 1928 Zev Jabotinsky wrote in *The Goals of the Zionist Revisionists*: "The first goal of Zionism is to create a Hebrew majority on both sides of the Jordan River." The assumptions in the article are: "The Jewish people possess an incontrovertible historical right to the land of Israel according to the promise of the God of Israel." Jabotinsky taught that the Jewish people had acquired rights to the country since it had formed the cradle of Jewish national life and was the source from which Jewish culture developed. Those are the basic assumptions of the Herut party in the Knesset. It is the party that advocates the annexation of the territories acquired by arms in 1967.

Somewhere in between there is a great body of Zionists who, if they are in Israel, will fight to the last drop of their blood to defend their country and, if they are outside Israel, will fight to the last drop of the blood of the people of Israel – and dip into their own pockets – to keep Israel secure. But at the same time they are aware that Israel's militant policies may, in the long run, destroy Israel. They would be willing to compromise for a peaceful settlement.

thirteen

An Industrious People

MANY OF US, IN OUR COMPASSION FOR THE POOREST OF THE refugee people and our concern to persuade our readers to use their influence to do something to help, have distorted the picture.

I have made up my mind many times to concentrate on the "successful" refugees, on some of the fifteen hundred doctors and scientists and lawyers and professors scattered around the world. The Palestinian research people claim they have over fifty thousand university graduates; and the universities in Damascus, Beirut, Cairo, and Amman all have large quotas of refugee students. Many of the professors are Palestinians too.

When I meet a Palestinian refugee outside a camp – and often I find them in the camps too – I take for granted he will speak English and probably French. I have often been humbled by their fluency in languages, their depth of culture, and sometimes I feel uncouth, so great is their innate courtesy and hospitality. The cultured Arab is one of the world's most civilized men.

When I returned to the Middle East in 1968 I was conscious of the distortion of the Arab image for which churchmen and the church press and fund-raisers have been partly responsible. We had heard enough about those tired mothers with hungry and sick children living on the meagre charity of the world, waiting for the UN to settle their problems and let them go home again.

But I soon discovered that it was the "poor refugee" who commanded my attention. Whether the children of these mistreated people solve the problem in their rebellious and revolutionary way or whether the world through the UN or the Big Four or the Big Two finds a peaceful way, there won't be peace until the poor refugee gets a decent chance to live a decent life in his own land.

But it should be remembered that sixty per cent of the refugees have made it somehow on their own outside the camps.

And most of those who haven't made it have tried. Even those within the camps usually have their diet supplemented by some members of the family working for them.

The present Commissioner General of UNRWA, Mr. Laurence Michelmore, said:

"Every indication is [the refugees] are industrious. The children are eager for an education. Their parents are determined they will have it. After the [1967] war when we asked what they wanted most, the thing they mentioned first was 'school.' When they have training they are eager to find a job; and if a man or boy finds a job he takes it and begins immediately to support his family."

Dr. John Davis, former Commissioner General, wrote in *The Evasive Peace*,

"By nature the Palestinian Arabs are a friendly and an orderly people. They are also an innately industrious people – not withstanding the impression to the contrary that a casual observer might gain from visiting a large refugee camp – following the upheaval of 1948, virtually all able-bodied refugees who possessed skills . . . found jobs almost immediately and became self-supporting."

One day I showed a just-off-the-press copy of the *United Church Herald* to Muneer Sabbagh, a Palestinian friend of mine in Beirut. He would be pleased, I assumed, with a story of mine the editor had published about refugees.

Muneer was not pleased. Although he is one of the gentlest men I have ever known, he showed mild irritation. "There you go again," he said, "giving the world the impression we are helpless people living in tents." He was right.

But to be self-supporting the Palestinian refugees have had to scatter all over the world. Jordan accorded them citizenship and many achieved citizenship in other countries. But Jordan could not provide opportunities for them all, so the Palestinians have become the new Jews of the new diaspora of the Middle East.

They are not the kind of people who are beaten by their suffering. They have not responded by going away quietly and losing themselves elsewhere in the Arab world.

The orderliness of the camps and the lack of delinquency among the Palestinian youth are startling facts of life for the westerner, troubled by conditions among North American young people.

"We have no juvenile delinquency," I was told by camp leaders. I was told the same again by UNRWA and church people. "No . . . come to think of it we don't have juvenile delinquency."

Dr. John Davis wrote:
"The refugee camps have never been harassed by hooliganism or unruly bands of youth with idle hours on their hands – not even in the Gaza Strip where employment opportunities are minimal."

Arab intellectuals are, depending upon their emotional make-up, depressed, frustrated, and infuriated by naive western acceptance of the Israeli claims clichéd in the propaganda phrase "making the desert bloom like the rose." I have been told by two distinguished Canadians, one a cabinet minister and the other an able broadcaster, that although they had visited only one side, "We saw the other side from the air. Israel was green. Jordan was brown."

This is comparable to flying over North America and discovering that Canada is muskeg, rocks, and lakes, and the US is a vast cultivated garden.

There is desert and wasteland in both Israel and Jordan. There are orchards and vineyards in both. The Israelis have done well with their part. They have received more economic aid than any people in the world in relation to their size and population. America itself has contributed 3.6 billion dollars in direct aid, plus more than another billion in tax-free gifts. And, according to the 1951 report of the Palestine Conciliation Commission of the UN, four-fifths of Israel's area and two-thirds of her cultivable land belonged to Palestine refugees prevented from returning home. One-third of Israel's Jewish population was living on absentee Arab property; nearly one-third of the new Jewish immigrants were settled in urban areas abandoned by Arabs. Half the citrus orchards, almost all of the olive groves, and ten thousand shops, businesses, and stores in Israel in 1953 belonged to absentee Palestine refugees.

I have been amused and irritated at the "oh's" and "ah's" of Christian pilgrims, being shown about by expert Israeli guides, at the beautiful Israeli orchards – all wrested from the desert one would think. Yet as a farmer I know something about how quickly trees grow.

One need only give a little attention to what the travellers said about Palestine before Zionism or spend a little time in Lebanon to sense the enormity of the propaganda trick that has been played upon us.

Mark Twain described the rich green valleys of the Huleh district in North Galilee a century ago. Sir Moses Montefiore wrote in 1839: "In the Holy Land the Jewish settlers will find a greater certainty of success; here they will find wells already dug, olives and vines already planted and a land so rich as to require little manure."

In the mid-thirties I was required to read Sir George Adams Smiths', *An Historical Geography of the Holy Land*. He wrote: "If Palestine be not a land of forests, it is a land of orchards. . . ." And in 1911, Ellsworth Huntington, an eminent American geographer, described Palestine as: "The fertile, well-watered strip of the Philistine coastal plain." He added:

"The modern Arab fellah like the peasant of the past, raises his grains with no water except that furnished by the rains, but for oranges, lemons and other valuable crops, he must have moisture during the long dry summer. Accordingly he digs numerous wells, and from them obtains a continual supply by means of pumps."

I have great respect for the able, industrious Israelis who have done great things in the deserts. But it is false and unfair to imply to the world that the Palestinian had done little for himself. There is great backwardness, there is illiteracy, there are old-fashioned farming methods in the Arab world. But that is only part of the story.

In Kuwait I was met by a Palestinian employee of the Consolidated Contractors Corporation who drove me from the airport in an air-conditioned car to an air-conditioned hotel.

I asked him about conditions.

"I ask myself, 'What's a man want in life?' And I say, 'He wants a good job with decent pay, a good school for his children, and in case he has bad luck some sort of medical insurance and good doctors and hospitals.' Here we have them all. I'm happy," he told me.

He was one of the lucky Palestinians you find all over the fast-developing Arab world. Without the Palestinians Kuwait would collapse. They provide the technicians, the engineers, the trained and educated workers to make the oil economy boom. But only a few of them are citizens and citizenship in Kuwait is hard to come by.

I didn't find the Palestinians complaining. Home to them is still Palestine and most of those I met had families back in Jordan, Syria, or Lebanon. Much of their pay goes back to parents and children, brothers and sisters in Jordan, Lebanon, or Syria. And each week there is a deduction from every Palestinian abroad to be sent to equip and maintain their unofficial army – the fedayeen.

This, of course, is part of the great tragedy, that so much of the initiative and industry of the Arabs and the Israelis is spent on a wasteful military struggle in a part of the undeveloped world where initiative and industry are so badly needed.

If a just settlement could be achieved, if the Israelis and Arabs of the future could work together in peace, then the roses really could be made to bloom. For the potential wealth is enormous. A part of the world that cradled early civilization and gave birth to the three great monotheistic religions could prosper again.

fourteen

The Economic Refugees

MR. KAMEL ABDULRAHMAN IS A PALESTINE REFUGEE, AN EN-gineer and a wealthy, successful, and attractive man. He is the head of a big Arab construction company called The Consolidated Contractors Corporation. The CCC does work in Libya, Kuwait, Jordan, Saudi Arabia, and several other Arab countries. The senior partners and many of the employees in the firm are Palestine refugees too.

Mr. Abdulrahman is typical of many Palestinians who have not only done very well for themselves but have done well for other Palestinians. For one thing, Mr. Abdulrahman likes to employ Palestine refugees, and he says the best employees he has in his firm are the young men who were economic refugees. One reason, he says, is "they have character." He says character is particularly important in the construction industry when a man goes away from home to work among strangers.

Now, what's an economic refugee? He is a Palestinian who, when the country was partitioned, lost his fields and his source of livelihood but did not lose his house. Many Palestinians lived in border villages whose lands were placed in Israel by the partition or were lost to Israel during the fighting. Most Arab farmers live in villages and go out to tend their fields. Those Palestinians who lost *everything* become the responsibility of the United Nations Relief and Works Agency. But technically the economic refugees were not refugees and had no claim on UNRWA, so life for them was hard. This was one of the areas where the numerous voluntary agencies of the

Middle East were able to help; some of the UN agencies stretched the point a bit too.

One day I visited one of the border villages called Qubiebeh, a few kilometers southwest of Jerusalem. It and the surrounding villages are poor and some of the people are illiterate. Until the late sixties there was a death rate among new-born babies of up to thirty per cent. Then, following the June war, the Near East Christian Council of Churches started a project in Qubiebeh which has brought about a revolution in the area. When I got there a large waiting room was filled with mothers and teen-aged sisters holding babies. In the kitchen food was being prepared to be eaten at little tables in the next room. After the morning meal young nursing assistants go out to visit the homes of the people to help the mothers wash and feed their children. There is a regular weighing-in programme and after a time the programme sells itself when the mothers see their children gaining weight.

Sometimes I have been a bit annoyed and troubled by the rather disreputable clothing church people in North America give for clothing drives for refugees. In the Qubiebeh project such old clothes are put to good use. The cast-offs from the used clothing boxes are repaired or made over.

Some of the graduates from the school had already been hired as teachers. More important than that, in some communities, as soon as a girl gets home from a morning at school, the neighbour women gather round to have her teach them what she has learned that day.

Later I went to see another NECC project among the refugees of the same sort, only on the other side of the river in Amman. The superintendent, Mrs. Leila Jirys, showed me the clinic where pregnant mothers were being given vitamin pills, mothers with new babies were receiving powdered milk and other nutritional supplements. In one room a group of twenty teen-aged girls were eating the lunch they had just cooked themselves. It was made of rice, beans, and tomatoes. Each day a different dish is prepared and cooked and the girls are taught how to use foods that are inexpensive, native, in season, and nutritious. Those girls told me they liked sewing classes best. For one thing, they didn't have to eat what they sewed.

Most of these refugees did not live in camps and this is one of the common misunderstandings of the refugee work in the Middle East. About sixty per cent of the refugees and displaced persons are not and never have been in refugee camps. And even the camps are not camps in the ordinary sense of the word. They do not have wire or gates and do not in any way inhibit people from coming and going as they wish.

One of the main activities of the voluntary agencies working with the refugees is loaning them money. Many Palestinians left the West Bank after the June war because they had been ruined financially and couldn't start into business again with their funds frozen in the bank. The Jordan banks were closed in June, 1967, and kept closed. Israel opened branches among the Arab communities but many small operators couldn't get loans or they wouldn't pay the nine percent interest rate.

The World Council of Churches and other agencies working among the refugees have always emphasized the self-help programmes. The Palestinians are an ingenious people with considerable imagination and flair for business. The Moslem is by religion opposed to usury, as Christians and Jews once were, "and he is sure opposed to paying the nine percent interest that the banks charge," one of them told me.

Mr. Elias Khoury, whose wife superintends the operation for the NECC at Qubiebeh, was responsible for the handling of the loans to Arabs in Jerusalem. He told me:

"We have made sixty-two loans totalling about twenty thousand dollars and sixty-one of them are being paid off regularly. Shoemakers, carpenters, tailors, barbers, that kind of little business man borrows from us and they don't borrow very much for they are so uncertain about the future. The shoemakers are doing all right now, for Arab prices are lower than Israeli prices so even the Israeli Jews come to the Arab shoemakers. But the carpenters are having it bad, for following the June war construction in the Arab world came to an end."

While I was sitting in the office someone came in for a small loan to operate a paint and body shop. The repairman had always got his compressed air from a nearby service station, but the service station was forced out of business – when the Israelis blew up a house next door – and so the repairman needed to buy equipment himself. The Council of Churches loaned him four hundred dollars.

Joe Thompson, Director of The Lutheran World Federation's Relief programme on the East Bank of the Jordan following the June war and prior to that in Jerusalem, told me, rather inelegantly, I thought, for a devout Lutheran, "most of these refugees aren't even in the camps and those who are aren't sitting on their fannies. They are using their initiative and we are just trying to help them help themselves. That's something I hope you can get across to the people back home."

No refugee worker likes the hand-out stuff, necessary though it was and at times still is. What they like to do is to help a depressed people help themselves, whether that means capital for a bakery, for a school to teach a skill, or for equipment to do a job.

fifteen

When an Arab Village
Is Bombed

ONE DAY IN AMMAN I ATTENDED A COMMITTEE MEETING OF the Volags, the representatives of the voluntary agencies who work among the Palestinian refugees on the East bank. There were CARE and the Save the Children Fund, UNRWA, YW and YMCA, Mennonites, Catholic Relief Services, The Near East Council of Churches, The Lutheran World Federation, and others. They were having a discussion about making cement blocks. The question was, would it be better to have the cement blocks made locally in a small town where there was unemployment or to buy them, probably for less money, from a big contractor.

I wondered what they wanted cement blocks for anyway, but it was explained to me that the agencies were busy helping people in bombed villages rebuild their homes. At that time I didn't even know there were bombed villages in Jordan.

I learned that up in the north-east, not far from the ancient ruins of Jerash, about fifteen villages were being regularly shelled by the Israelis from the Golan Heights, or bombed by their planes. The Jordanians charged that the Israelis were trying to drive them out of what was a very rich agricultural area and they had made up their minds to stay. The Israelis said it was in reprisal for commando attacks on their kibbutzim south of Galilee.

Eventually the committee decided that an Arab representative of the Lutheran World Federation ought to drive up to the villages and see how things were getting along. Naim Aweideh, the Lutheran worker, took me along for the ride.

We went to the village of Kufor Assad where cement blocks were being made in a small hand machine owned by CARE, but loaned to UNRWA, who loaned it to the Near East Christian Council of Churches. That's the way the Volags work in east Jordan. Somebody's always loaning something to somebody else or giving something to somebody to help someone else. On our way we stopped at another village where the Lutheran World Federation was providing materials for the people to build a new school. Aweideh, who was an expert agriculturalist in Palestine before he became a refugee, was able to point out all sorts of interesting agricultural oddities to me along the way, for a great deal of experimentation is going on in Jordan. "He won't make any money out of oranges there," he would say. "He should plant olives."

At the edge of Kufor Assad we found three men making blocks. They had water stored in drums that had originally contained used clothing shipped from America. They shovelled the cement into the little machine and set the blocks. It was a very simple operation. I watched them for awhile and then wandered across the field to where children were having classes in the open. Their school had been shelled and burned. Nearby the ground was black, where shelling had hit a farmer's threshing floor and his crop had burned. Then we went on into the village to survey the damage there. Fortunately, air raid shelters had been dug and, although several houses had had direct hits, most of the people were down below at the time; only one person in Kufor Assad had been killed recently. They showed me a place where a dud bomb had been dropped from a plane. Although it didn't go off it wrecked the mud brick house it had fallen on. Another, nearby, had crashed through the roof of the house and exploded, leaving a big hole where the floor had been. I went down into one of the air raid shelters, which was piled with blankets and was obviously being used for sleeping. When I came up I asked a lad who was there, "When did you use that last," and he looked at his watch and said, "Ten minutes ago." Apparently, while we had been out watching the cement block making or driving along in the car, we had not heard a plane going over but the village children had. They had been taught to scurry into a shelter whenever a plane appeared.

A few days after that I wanted to cross the Jordan to Israel to spend some time in Jerusalem. There was a big flap on for an Arab bomb had been let off in a supermarket, killing a number of Arabs and Israelis. My crossing of the bridge was delayed one day. When I reached Jerusalem I asked one of my Arab friends about the market-place bombing and his comment was, "All responsible people are against that sort of thing. But did you know that it was a reprisal for the Israelis blowing up a house at Nablus?" I hadn't heard that, but his story was to the effect that when a home, suspected of hiding weapons or a member of a commando group, had been dynamited by the Israelis a sick girl in the house had been killed; so in vengeance for that the Arabs had set off the bomb in the market-place. At least, that was the Arab side of it. (I later heard it was a reprisal for an Israeli bombing of Irbid.)

I went back from there to Beirut. A few weeks later there was a report on the front page of Beirut's *Daily Star* that the village of Kufor Assad had been bombed by the Israelis as a reprisal for the Jerusalem market-place bombing. There had been a direct hit on a shelter; fourteen were killed and eighteen injured. The *Star* carried pictures of the bodies of three small children dug out of the shelter. It was indicated that the attack may have been aimed at Iraqis who were hiding out in the hills near Kufor Assad. Mr. Yoon Gu Lee, the Secretary of the Near East Council of Churches for refugee work, told me he was going over to see Kufor Assad because he had heard that one of the new houses the NECC was building out of the cement blocks had been hit. I had learned that it was not always good business to quote what one saw in the newspapers of the Middle East so I went along with Mr. Lee to see what a little village would look like after it had a going over.

We found the whole place a shambles. About thirty-five hundred people live in Kufor Assad and the houses are built of stones and dirt and many are plastered with dried cow dung; eighty-three were destroyed and another sixty-three damaged. It was raining hard and the cow dung was slippery and the unpaved streets were deep in sticky mud. Some of the children followed me and Mr. Lee through the streets, gazing curiously and rather cheerfully, it seemed to me, at the rubble of their school. There were no men about but I discovered later they were in the mosque for prayers. Digging out and clearing up work was temporarily halted.

We and the children looked with interest at what was left of the girls' school subsidized by the Near East Christian Council. Rockets had made direct hits. The furniture, much of it splintered, had been piled in one room that was only partially destroyed, but all the windows were broken and the rain was going in. Some rather tame doves were perched in the broken olive trees in front of the school. This, with my Biblical background, seemed to symbolize something. There would be no more school for awhile in Kufor Assad, for the boys' school had been destroyed in the earlier raid and it wasn't possible during the rainy season to have school outside.

While we were looking about in the almost deserted village a great flock of men suddenly poured out of the mosque and came down the street. Many of them were soldiers, Iraqis and Jordanians, and commandos in their camouflage dress. They were suspicious of me but reassured by the presence of Mr. Lee, who was a Korean. Koreans are more to be trusted in these times than someone who looks like an American. I asked what the sermon had been about. "The situation, not the Koran," I was told grimly. They wanted to know what my camera was doing. Things got a little tense but we were taken to the mukhtar of the village, who had good English, and he told me I could take whatever pictures I liked. "Canadians haven't a very good name over here either," the Anglican rector of the church in nearby Irbid told me, for North Americans are blamed for supplying planes that bomb these defenseless villages.

Irbid and Kufor Assad are situated in one of most strategic parts of the Jordan. The valley is full of citrus orchards and the plains around produce wheat and other cereals. A huge irrigation project had been stopped by the Israeli attacks on the Ghor Canal and tons of equipment were standing idle. "These raids have completely paralyzed our economy. The people are afraid to go down into the valley to harvest fruit or tend the irrigation," the Rev. Akel Akel of Irbid told me. There were Iraqi and Jordanian troops in the area, as well as commandos. If the attacks on the villages were meant to hit the commandos they were wasted. The camouflaged camps are seen from the roadside, safely tucked into the caves which are plentiful in the valleys and gulleys of that area of Jordan. They are not good targets. The Arabs insist that the Israeli raids and shelling are really meant to intimidate and drive them out, as the Syrians to the north had been driven out.

The day after the raid the Israelis unveiled a new scheme for a Jewish settlement of the Syrian Heights. The plan, according to the government spokesman in Israel, was to establish twenty-five settlements, with between ten to fifteen thousand Jewish immigrants, in the area. This was completely contrary to Article 49 of the Geneva Convention. The Jordanian Arabs, seeing what happened a few miles away when their Syrian brethren fled in panic, told me they were determined not to leave. Fourteen other villages in the area have also been hit repeatedly and the volunteer agencies have been unable to keep up with the rebuilding. Most of those killed and injured in such raids are children, women, and old people, because the Arab men weren't in the villages during the military "exchanges." In Kufor Assad four little children were killed outright; one twenty-one year old girl was in hospital, her spine so injured she would never walk again.

There was an irony about that direct hit on the shelter, for about fifty feet from it a new two-family house erected by the church agency rebuilding project had not been touched. Mr. Lee arranged for small gifts of money to go to the victims who were in hospital, but the rebuilding programme would require more funds than the agency could provide or perhaps even risk in such an exposed area.

Villages such as Kufor Assad don't get assistance from UNRWA for the villagers aren't refugees, they are Jordanian citizens. They and their ancestors have lived in such villages for many centuries. Mr. Lee asked the head man what the Near East Council could do to help in the emergency and he said that the Jordanian government was looking after them and added, "Just tell everybody we're staying; we've asked the government to build us better air raid shelters." However, one family obviously wasn't going to stay in Kufor Assad. They were packing their household goods in a panel truck in the rain. "They're refugees," the head man told us disdainfully. "They don't really belong to Kufor Assad."

We went back from there to Irbid to have our lunch at the Anglican rectory with Mr. and Mrs. Akel. The city of Irbid had been raided three nights in a row also, but the damage was less. One of the hospitals had been hit. Somehow or other hospitals and churches seem to attract bombs like magnets. The main attack for the three nights had been, it was reported from Tel Aviv, against the Iraqi army units. The Israelis said that the attack on Irbid was in reprisal for the Iraqi shelling of Israeli Jordan valley villages. Mrs. Akel told me that Irbid had had five air raid alarms. "It's just swish and then a bang," she said. "We haven't had much sleep lately," she added.

"The last time I was here after a raid there was blood all over this street," Mr. Yoon Gu Lee told me. At that time there were sixty killed and about a hundred and eighty wounded. I hadn't heard about it and was interested and a little frustrated to note that the Western press I saw hadn't carried the story of Kufor Assad. About ten days later I was back in Jerusalem and saw an article in the Jerusalem Post criticizing a British paper for carrying a story of the Kufor Assad attack and the picture of the dead children. The British paper was charged with being anti-Semitic for carrying such things. It was implied that the picture was a fake. It was no fake.

I often wonder why the Western press has tended to ignore these Israeli attacks by plane on civilians in Jordan while they give so much space to commando attacks on Israel.

During the years since 1967 Israel's effective bombardment by plane and shell has turned vast areas of the richest Arab land into unproductive and uninhabitable no-man's land. The theory seems to be to surround her newly-acquired territories with desert, to protect her security and to force the Arabs into signing a peace treaty on Israeli terms.

What this does for Israeli security I don't know. What it does to Arab attitudes is obvious. You don't pound a proud people into submission – especially when there are so many millions of them.

sixteen

What Happened
on the Golan Heights

ISRAEL'S CONQUEST OF SYRIA'S GOLAN HEIGHTS WAS NAKED aggression. When the objective history of the 1967 war is written, it will emerge as one of the most cynical military conquests of modern times. Israel defied the UN Security Council, flouted the Geneva Conventions, ignored the Charter of the United Nations, conquered a major city after having agreed to a cease fire, emptied eighty villages of their people, and, having driven out the native civilians, proceeded to settle the area with its own people and exploited its resources.

In the year that followed my visit to Lake Mzerib I often wondered what had happened to the displaced persons of Syria. There were lots of stories about the Syrian bunkers overlooking Galilee, which had become a major tourist attraction for visitors to Israel. But there were no reports about the hundred and thirty-eight thousand Syrians who had fled before, during, or after the fighting from Kuneitra and the villages round about.

I went back to Damascus, where I found the most intense hostility to Israel in all the hostile Middle East. Church leaders and representatives of the international agencies were almost as bitterly anti-Israel as the refugees. The reasons were many. Among them were the harsh measures taken by Israeli occupation forces against the Syrians who had remained behind in the conquered area. Another was Israel's complete refusal to permit any Syrians, even for the most urgent compassionate reasons, to return to their former homes. The complete flouting of the provisions of the Geneva Convention of August 12, 1949, which Israel had signed, had not only embittered the Syrian DP's but had angered the international community.

In both Jordan and Egypt it had become possible, after a time, for many families who had been separated during the hostilities to be reunited. But not so in occupied Syria. I found that seven hundred and thirty-nine Syrians had applied on compassionate grounds through the International Red Cross to return to the Occupied Territories. Not a single one had been permitted to go back.

At that time, October 1968, the Red Cross was searching for two hundred and thirty six missing soldiers and two hundred and sixty-three missing civilians, but none had been found. The Red Cross and Red Crescent people believed they were dead. Some of the missing were sons and husbands taken from their families in the middle of the night by Israeli patrols following the June war. This was a technique used by the Israelis to empty a village. "When that knock on the door in the middle of the night happens once or twice in a village, the rest of the families pack up and head for safety in destitution across the border," a Syrian school teacher who had lived in such a village told me.

The Israelis had completely razed some Syrian villages in the Golan. Graves were found where it was suspected some of the "missing" had been buried, but because of Israeli health regulations they could not be opened. That regulation may have been a valid one but it was another cause for bitterness among the Syrians.

The methods used by the Israelis to "persuade" the Syrians to leave their homes in Occupied Territories and go to Damascus were clever, intimidating, and effective, and they were contrary to international law. It is against international law to remove civilians from an area which has come under a military occupation, and it is contrary to international law to settle your own people there.

Israel immediately set out without any secrecy whatever to settle the Golan Heights with Jewish citizens.

One international representative told me that he arrived one day at the frontier during the first year of occupation when he wasn't expected, and saw things he wasn't supposed to see. He was man-handled by Israelis back into his car, which had clearly been marked with the sign of his organization, and an Israeli machine gun was pointed at him. Later he made strong protests about it and the officer responsible was removed. "But I thought then," he said, "if they would treat me that way, what must they do to frighten the defenseless Arabs?" He told me that most Israeli officers and soldiers were humane in their conduct and easy to get along with, but he added that while some were very kind to the Arabs, the original Israeli military governor, Akeeba Weinstein, hated them. After heavy pressure from the International Red Cross Weinstein was replaced. Weinstein, it is said, had been captured and tortured by the Syrians in 1940.

Actually, one application for repatriation through the Red Cross was approved but the return was never carried out. In the panic of the June war a blind man and his wife fled, leaving behind his semi-crippled mother and her aged sister in Kuneitra. Later they asked to be allowed to return so they could look after one another. The application was approved; it was the only one. "So that couple made their way from Damascus to the frontier where they were told the papers hadn't arrived and they would have to come back later. They went back to Damascus and later returned; but it was the same story. Four times the blind man and his wife made their way from Damascus to the frontier and four times they were turned back." Then one day an international representative saw the two old ladies, the semi-crippled mother and her aged sister, trudging across the four kilometers of no-man's land on their way to join the blind son and his wife in Damascus.

One can hear a thousand similar stories from the refugees, and many may be exaggerated, but the stories I report are from non-Syrian sources or have been confirmed by international representatives, or I have followed them through myself. Such charges have been documented and made at the UN by Dr. George Tomeh, Syria's highly respected and scholarly ambassador.

Before the 1967 war Kuneitra and its surrounding suburbs

had been a city of approximately thirty thousand. I was told by one Red Cross representative that on Sunday the 11th of June, there were about four hundred people still in Kuneitra and probably another four hundred people were in hiding. In other words, something like eight hundred when the Israelis took over. By mid-1970, when I visited, there were four Arabs left in the city. The Israelis have a kibbutz in the old Syrian Officers Club.

I go into some of this because it has been said that the Syrians presented the attacking Israelis with a completely empty country. That is not true. Thousands were driven out later by the Israelis. It is not contrary to international law for civilians to leave a battle area in the face of an attacking army. It *is* illegal to drive a people out or to refuse to let them back after a conquest.

One of the questions still asked is this: How many did Israel uproot and drive out one way or another? The present Governor of the district of Kuneitra, in Damascus, says that there were a hundred and thirty-eight thousand people on the Golan Heights prior to the June war. There are eight thousand there now, most of them Druse. He says that thirty-five per cent of the people left between the fifth and the tenth and that on June 10th there were still twelve thousand people in the Kuneitra area. By June 15th there were five thousand; by July 15th, two thousand; and by August 15th, six hundred and fifty, This was down to one hundred and fifty by November 10th, 1967; down to a hundred in February of 1968; fifty in May of 1968; and by the first of January 1970, eleven.

When the UN cease-fire was finally acted upon partially, there were people in most of the villages to the south of Golan. By the end of 1968 there were only twelve persons left in the eighty villages and a short time after they were entirely emptied. There are about eight thousand in the northern villages. Those who remained behind in the north are probably the best off, although they may be rather lonely, in all of the occupied territory. Most of them are Druse, and the Druses get along better with the Israelis than Moslems or Christians. They have always been a minority and they have become skilled at adapting themselves to whomever is in power.

In Damascus I met some Syrians in late 1968 who had

stuck it out in Kuneitra for about sixteen months of the occupation before they finally left. They told me at that time there were still fourteen people left in the city. "We have no hope of ever getting back," one of them said. "The Palestinians were promised for twenty years that they could return, and look at them."

Why did the Israelis treat the Syrians so harshly? "The Syrians were the only Arabs the Israelis ever demeaned themselves to hate," the Red Cross representative told me. Incident followed incident, some trivial, some fatal, in the Galilee area all through the years. The Syrians had the advantage of being able to shoot and shell from the heights above down on the Israeli kibbutzim and settlements below. Innocent Jews died. The Israelis continued to break the agreements with the UN and constantly encroached on the rich bottom land of the demilitarized zone.

I used to take at face value the Israeli charges of Syrian shelling and sniping of their Galilee kibbutzim until I heard UN and other informed people tell the other side of the story.

A study of the UN reports of that troubled area is edifying. A popular but highly informed story, Major-General Carl von Horn's *Soldiering for Peace*, helps one understand the Syrian position. General von Horn was Commander of the UN peace-keeping force in Palestine from 1958 to 1960.

In Lieutenant-General E. L. M. Burns' *Between Arab and Israeli*, there are other documented reports on the Syrian-Israeli problems. General Burns was Chief of Staff of the UN peace-keeping force from August 1954 until November 1956.

These informed experts don't suggest the Israelis were all wrong and the Syrians all right in the struggles over the years. But the Israelis played a lot of cute little tricks in their attempt to appropriate Syrian territory.

Back in June 1967, if the UN had not acted, Israel could have taken Damascus with little opposition. She still could. Instructions were issued to the Damascus civilians by the advancing Israelis on how to act when the Israelis came – hang their white flags out the windows and so on. It sounded realistic enough to the Damascus people when they saw the Syrian Army retreating to the north.

Rumours still linger in Syria of a high-level sell-out to the Israelis by the army.

In Jerusalem Anwar Nuseibeh, Jordan's former minister of Defence and one time Ambassador to London, asked me in May 1970 if I knew what had happened to the Syrian army, that it gave up so quickly. I didn't know and assumed it was a rhetorical question and he was going to tell me.

"I don't know either," he said. "I have often wondered, for it was believed to be a damn good army."

Later I asked the Kuneitra Governor and his public relations spokesman, who were both in Kuneitra at the time. He told me, "We were beaten from the air. We heard the last anti-aircraft guns silenced. The Arab forces weren't equal to it." I got the impression from them and other Syrian officials that the army fled to save itself. Dr. Tomeh implied that Syria could have held the Israelis back for a day or two, but at the cost of destruction of the army. And the regime needed the army to hold itself in power in Damascus.

When the Israelis announced a Five-Year Plan to expand the Israeli settlement in the Golan Heights on May 31st, 1970, Ambassador Tomeh made a statement to the General Assembly, reviewing some of the resolutions of June 1967.

He informed them of "an additional and most recent outrageous development." He reported that "the Jewish Telegraph Agency on June 1, 1970, published this item: date-lined Jerusalem, 31 May.

" 'A $48 million five-year plan to expand Israeli settlements in the occupied Golan Heights was approved by the Ministry of Agriculture's planning committee today. The project calls for the addition of six new settlements to the eleven already established in the region. Each settlement will have 1,000 head of cattle and about 8,000 acres of land for grazing. Golan settlements already produce potatoes, citrus fruits, plums, olives and walnuts.' "

Mr. Tomeh proceeded to remind the Assembly of what Israel had done *after* both Israel and Syria had accepted the cease-fires of June 6, June 7, and June 11th, 1967.

On June 11th the Security Council called for "the prompt return to the cease-fire positions of any troops which have moved forward subsequent to 1630 hours on June 10."

The fact is while Israel and Syria were both agreeing to the UN orders to cease fire, Israel kept right on going until she occupied what she wanted of Syria.

After that the UN voted repeatedly, demanding that Israel permit the return of those civilians who had fled during the hostilities. Israel ignored such demands and the UN has done nothing about it.

The displaced persons are still out. And Israel, contrary to the Charter of the United Nations, Article 2, paragraph 4, which prohibits any member of the UN from using force against the territorial integrity of any State, proceeds to settle her own people on the land of others.

A few weeks after the Israeli triumph of June 1967, Israel issued an invitation to Jewish people in other parts of the world to come and settle on the empty heights of Golan. Michael Comay told me in August 1967 that Israel could settle five hundred thousand people on the heights. I argued about the pathetic peasants whom I had seen in their camps and in the open without shelter, and his comment was, "Syria is an underpopulated country. They can easily absorb another hundred thousand." This is correct. But it is not the point. So could Canada and the USA absorb more people. Mr. Yigal Allon, one of the leaders of the Jewish terrorist organizations before 1948 and now Deputy Premier, said in a speech in early August 1967 that the heights belong to Israel because they had belonged to Israel in ancient times. "Jephthah judged there," Allon said, basing Israeli claims to the land on a temporary possession more than three thousand years before.

One day in 1969 I stood with a young Israeli guide and a group of Canadian tourists at the north of the Sea of Galilee. The guide was an intelligent and attractive girl and, as so many are, extremely nationalist. She and I had an argument about my habit of speaking of "the occupied territories" and her habit of calling them "conquered territories." She was explaining the problems which Israel and Syria had had over the years and why there had been so much shooting around Galilee –

always disturbing or fascinating for Jewish tourists and Christian pilgrims.

"Some of you may think the June war started with Egypt down in the south," she said, "over the Gulf of Aqaba and the Straits of Tiran. Well, it started here over water. The trouble has always been over the possession of the sources of water."

She grinned at me and said, "Does that suit you?" I told her I thought it wasn't bad.

You will find nowhere in recent history a more cynical and successful carrying out of a long-term expansionist policy than that Israel has waged against Syria.

Some of the facts in the earlier part of this chapter about the refusal of Israel to permit refugees from the heights to return to join their families were printed in an article I wrote in late 1968 for several church magazines. Before publishing it I showed it to a senior official in the American Embassy in Beirut. "You are right of course," he said, "but you're going to catch hell." When I sent it to my own magazine I asked one of my colleagues to send a copy to the International Red Cross in Geneva so he could be prepared when he began to "catch hell" for me. He did and the Red Cross of course confirmed it. After all Geneva's sources and mine were much the same. But there was a fuss in Toronto and another in Geneva.

I had some satisfaction though, when a few months later Israel did permit about four hundred persons separated from their homes to go back to the Golan. Most of them were Druse. One Christian woman and her six children eventually got back. The other hundred and thirty thousand, as Michael Comay said, "are out." And as far as Israel is concerned they will not get back.

When the UN voted overwhelmingly to investigate the alleged atrocities in occupied territoriess in the autumn of 1968, the US and Canada abstained. I was in Syria shortly after and discussed it with Dr. Adib Daoudy, Under Secretary in Foreign Affairs, and an experienced diplomat at UN affairs for Syria. I asked why Syria did not agree to a settlement on the basis of the November 22nd, 1967, resolution of the Security Council. He said the main reasons were: "We believe Israel will stay where she is and seek to expand further. And Israel is a racist state. We see no difference between her and Rhodesia or South Africa but she has been accorded a different position by world opinion."

At the time Daoudy was irritated by the fact the US and Canada had abstained from voting on a "humanities" resolution that had just been taken at the UN calling for an investigation of alleged atrocities in occupied territories. "The US of course abstained for domestic political reasons. But why Canada – of all things on a humanities resolution favoured by almost the entire Assembly?"

Mr. Mitchell Sharp, Canada's Minister of External Affairs, explained to me that Canada had objected to the phrasing of the resolution, which already pre-judged the findings. Another significant detail might be added: Mr. Sharp represents a constituency in Parliament that has the second largest concentration of Jewish voters in Canada. When he was nominated by Mr. Philip Givens, a famous Canadian pro-Zionist, Givens reminded him, "This riding is fifty-two per cent Jewish and with us Israel is a gut issue."

The fact is, Mr. Sharp would be politically dead if he offended his Jewish voters. The only riding said to have a heavier concentration of Jewish votes in Canada is that of Prime Minister Pierre Elliot Trudeau. Mr. Trudeau would not suffer unduly if he offended his voters. He could always be given a "safe" seat elsewhere. But it is unlikely that Canada will take a very active role in Middle East affairs as long as Mr. Sharp is Minister of External Affairs.

Perhaps the simplest way to explain why the Golan Heights have been the object of cynical aggression is to quote from General Moshe Dayan from *Le Monde*, July 9th, 1969 – one of many similar statements made by the Israeli hero:

"People abroad ought to realize that quite apart from their strategic importance to Israel, Sinai, the Golan Heights, the Tiran Straits and the hills west of the Jordan lie at the heart of Jewish history! Nor has the 'restoration of historical Israel' ended yet. Since the return to Zion a hundred years ago a double process of colonization and expansion of frontiers has been going on. We have not yet reached the end of that road: It is the people of Israel who will determine the frontiers of their own state."

Back in the early years the Zionists made one claim after another for the whole of the headwaters country, supported by such influential figures as General Allenby and David Lloyd George.

The Council of Dutch Zionists demanded in 1918 that "the frontiers of Palestine – which they intended to make the new state of Israel – should extend to the east to the desert and in the north to points not far from Beirut and Damascus."

The experts of the British Foreign Office said:

" . . . a good case could be made for the extension of territory on economic grounds since Jewish colonization, if it were to be carried out without abruptly dislodging the native population, needed the large land reserves of the south and east and the waters of the north for irrigation purposes. The Zionists wanted to divert the Litani into the Jordan Valley and to set up a conservation scheme for all the waters flowing south and west from the Hermon."

On May 28th, 1970, I drove from Beirut to Southern Lebanon to the Arkoub area and the border village of Hebbariye. The Israelis had entered there a few days before when I was in Israel. They were censured by the UN Security Council for it. Then an Israeli school bus was shelled from across the Lebanese border. Some fedayeen condemned it as an irresponsible and criminal act. Some wondered why the Israelis would drive school buses along the frontier during hostilities. One small fedayeen group claimed, "We did it." The world condemned it.

The Lebanese officials could not give me permission or give security to me and other journalists to go into the Arkoub. "It's Fateh country," I was told. So I was accompanied by a second-year Fateh student from the American University of Beirut – a refugee from Jerusalem – who was concerned about an examination the next day.

99

Hebbariye was being shelled when we reached the edge of it and we were turned back and ordered to retire to a Fateh outpost on the mountain side. We listened to the shelling while some television people from Germany argued with the officials about going in to see the action and complained, correctly, that the Israelis would let the press and TV go into action with them. We had one casualty that afternoon. A young Fateh man carelessly shot himself and twenty-four young fedayeen almost panicked in their excitement. He was carried in with a bad thigh wound, covered with blood.

We listened to the BBC news of what was going on a mile or so away, over a car radio via Tel Aviv and London, and heard that the Israelis had crossed the border and presumed our hosts did not wish us to witness this little setback. Camouflaged armoured cars and tanks were hidden at the turns of the twisting road.

That night, back in Beirut, the Lebanese were wondering about another statement of Moshe Dayan's, made in October 1967: "Israel's borders, with the exception of that with Lebanon, are ideal."

About fifteen thousand new refugees had fled from the border and the Lebanese government had voted approximately ten million dollars to provide food and supplies. My young Fateh host told me this grant made the people of South Lebanon very angry. So they had a day's general strike. "They don't want food or money. They want to be protected, or at least given weapons to protect themselves," he said. But Lebanon can't protect her borders against Israel's modern weapons, techniques, and well-trained and dedicated soldiers and airmen. The Fateh can't protect them either. But the Fateh can melt into the mountains and when Israel withdraws seep back out again and harrass her some more.

I wondered, when I left, if the next time I visited Southern Lebanon I would go via Beirut or in an air-conditioned bus from Jerusalem.

seventeen

Life for Syrian Refugees

IN THE CENTRE OF DAMASCUS, IN "THE OLD CITY," MOST OF the city's Christians live. The chapel of Ananias, built in the very house, tradition says, where Paul was taken until he recovered from his blindness, is nearby. There is a church, too, where Paul was let down the wall in a basket to make his escape.

Through Pastor D. M. Mitry of the Syrian Evangelical (Presbyterian) Church I became acquainted with several of the Christian refugee families who fled from Kuneitra during the June 1967 war.

In one room off the courtyard of Mr. Mitry's church a widow and five children reside. Mrs. Ibrahim Barakat is an attractive, patient mother, who usually smiles. Her late husband was minister of the Presbyterian Church in Kuneitra. His father before him was a pastor in Tiberias on the Sea of Galilee.

The Barakats left Kuneitra with the other thousands when their city was bombed. He was unwell and shortly after he arrived in Damascus he died, leaving his wife and children without a home or means of support.

"He died a bitter man," Mr. Mitry told me. "He was a very good man, a truly religious man. He was consecrated, and did not concern himself with financial matters. He and I were like brothers – I feel responsible for his family."

Barakat had built a new church in Kuneitra and although the tiny congregation had paid him only a small salary – about fifty dollars a month – he had a brother who had gone abroad.

The brother helped and provided the money for the Barakats to build a house. But tragedy struck again. The brother across the seas died too and his gifts no longer came.

Mitry arranged for the family to live in one room of the old church. And the other twenty-five hundred Christians were also housed in rooms here and there or in church schools or other parts of the Orthodox, Catholic, and Protestant churches.

The government provided the equivalent of about five dollars a month per person.

The Barakat's children are bright and personable. Their education was upset though – one lad was taking a university course and the other was finishing his last year in high school.

The local Christian community was ready to help. "Our people are poor," Mitry says. What about outside help? Here I discovered that the regulations were in the way. World Council of Churches' funds went to provide new housing for thousands in tents. Discrimination in favour of Christians or special cases such as this was not permitted.

"I feel responsibility for these people living around here," Mitry often said to me. "You know, when a Catholic or Orthodox monk grows old or gets sick his church provides. I don't like to see anyone from the church living in poverty."

But round about Damascus there were thousands of non-Christian refugees living in worse conditions than the pastor's children. Help for them had to come first.

I last visited the Barakats in May 1970 and things were looking up a bit. The boys were in school, were getting work and helping out their mother. They still all lived in one room – but it looked as though they would make it. Fortunately for such families, in Syria's socialist state there are no university fees.

In early 1969 I visited a family named Haddad – they were Greek Orthodox and also from Kuneitra. There was a big collection of uncles and aunts and cousins.

Mrs. Fayez Haddad had one room and six small children – three boys and three girls. Her husband was still in Kuneitra, one of the eleven still sticking it out. She was hoping, and had been hoping for twenty months, to get back.

On Wednesday, the 7th of June, 1967, Fayez Haddad had put his wife and her five-day old baby into a truck and sent them off to Damascus. His elderly mother and five small children, and all the uncles and aunts and cousins, started on foot. Fayez said he would stay behind and keep shop, guarding extensive holdings against the inevitable havoc and looting when the soldiers came.

"What did you take with you?" I asked Mrs. Haddad.

"Nothing much," she said. "We expected to be going back in a few days."

She said that it took about four months to get a letter from her husband. "He can't say anything except he is well and he sends his greetings."

They both applied immediately through the Red Cross for the mother and family to go back. But none got back. Then in the winter of 1969 a few Druses got back. In the meantime Fayez was one of the last to stick it out. His wife had heard a little through other refugees who kept arriving from the occupied area. There was no trouble leaving. The Israelis encouraged that. It was just impossible to go back.

But Mrs. Haddad was still hopeful. "What will you do about school for the children in Kuneitra?" I asked her. "I was wondering about that," she said.

"What will happen if she doesn't get back?" I asked one of the male cousins. "Oh, eventually Fayez will have to give up and come here as we did. Then the Israelis will likely confiscate all his property."

One morning I had breakfast with one of the Haddad uncles. His wife set a good table, more than I needed but not good enough for her idea of Arab hospitality. "Some day I hope you can come back when we are back in our own home and then I can do my duty by you," she said. Then she started to cry.

"Those people had lovely homes and beautiful orchards and gardens back in Kuneitra," Mrs. Mitry told me.

Fourteen months later I was in Israel. I had heard that Mrs. Haddad and her children had finally received permission to return to Kuneitra – the only Christian family to make it. I decided to go see them and learned from the Red Cross where they lived – not in their Kuneitra home but in a northern village called Masada.

Masada is a lonely place for a Christian family. But they looked content. Fayez, a blacksmith, had work. They had not been permitted to remain in Kuneitra and the Israelis were trying to buy his property from him, but weren't offering nearly enough. He had been permitted to move his furniture to Masada.

"Next year we will send the three oldest children to a Christian school in Nazareth," he said. I told him that the school he named was Greek Catholic. "It doesn't matter," he said, "it is Christian." They are now attending a Druse school operated by the Israeli military governor.

He hopes in time to emigrate somewhere in the Western world – to Canada or the US or South America – to give the children a chance. It would be almost impossible for him to emigrate from Syria.

Back in Damascus I reported that I had seen the family and they were happy. Mrs. Haddad senior asked if I thought she should join them.

"If she got permission to go back, then she wouldn't ever see the rest of the family here," her granddaughter told me. "But if she stays here she will never see her son again. Poor grandmother, she cries all the time."

And it did seem rather sad and unnecessary. They are only thirty miles apart, but for the Syrians it is an uncrossable frontier.

Actually, one little Syrian with Red Cross help has made the crossing to Damascus and back. As far as I could find he is the only one of a hundred and thirty-eight thousand Syrians who has been able to cross and re-cross with Israeli permission.

In May 1970 little two-year old Samaan, son of Ibrahim Nasserallah and Jebard, his wife, made it – although his parents had to stay home.

It happened this way. The Nasserallahs live in the Druse village of Majdel Chams in the Northeast section of Occupied Syria. He is a teacher and they are the only Christians in the village.

Jebara had made a vow that if God would give her a son she would have him baptized in the ancient shrine of Seydnaya, a village north of Damascus. The Virgin, according to Greek Orthodox legend, appeared at Seydnaya, one of the East's oldest churches, back in the middle of the sixth century. A world-famous icon reputed to drip sacred oil with miraculous properties is kept in Seydnaya. It was much prized in Crusader times.

Orthodox mothers often make vows to have their babies baptized at Seydnaya, and the resident priest has many baptisms. On March 4th, 1968, a baby son was born at Majdel Chams. The church wasn't far away but there was a frontier with guards and an Occupying Power that would not let them come back if they were to leave for a baptism.

Although an Orthodox child is usually baptized between the fortieth and ninetieth days, there seemed no way. But there was that vow. So an application was made through the Red Cross and eventually, after many months, permission was granted. Little Samaan was taken to the Red Cross representative, who delivered him to waiting relatives from Damascus. On Friday, May 15th, 1970, the baby was immersed in the holy waters by Father Kalin Khoury while two hundred relatives and friends looked on.

eighteen

The Fedayeen

IN AMMAN A MOTHERLY HOUSEWIFE PREPARING SUNDAY dinner for the guests she brought home from the Anglican Church smiled her thanks when her African violets were admired. "I bought them from the Fateh auxiliary at Christmas," she explained. "They were selling them to raise money."

In the lobby of the UNESCO Palace during the World Conference of Christians at Beirut, attractive college students manned the Fateh booth, elbow to elbow with the Government Travel people, exhibits of Lebanese handwork, and the Red Crescent. A cute youngster – a sophomore from AUB – loaded interested visiting clergy with pamphlets and posters and introduced her grandfather, a distinguished retired pastor, once the Presbyterian minister of Galilee. I was given a free box of Fateh stationery, and was tempted to write notes to some of my more emotional Zionist friends in Toronto.

On a Thursday night in Damascus – the beginning of the Muslim weekend – the streets were jammed with fedayeen in camouflage uniforms and Syrian soldiers. And coming up from the Allenby Bridge a money-raising commando with a Czech automatic weapon and a book of raffle tickets accepted my left-over Israeli coins with a grin, saying he'd use them on his next trip across the Jordan.

It's difficult at first to get the Arab perspective. The "terrorists" of the North American and Israeli press are, in the Arab world, "Our boys." Those heroic Israeli soldiers are "the enemy."

106

In Occupied Territory, "the Arabs are not co-operating with the commandos," Mr. Schlomo Hillel, now head of the police, told me. "They are told to go back to their own side of the river if they want to fight."

"You should have asked him, 'Why are you blowing up our houses then?'" an Arab friend told me when I reported what Hillel had said. "Ninety per cent of the people are with them. It does create an embarrassment, though, for some. Out of their innate hospitality Arabs can't say 'no' to anyone who asks for shelter, even though it may mean trouble for them."

Hillel may have been partly right. The Israelis have got things under fair control in parts of "the New Territories of Israel," as some call them, but they must know that the whole population would turn on the Occupier if given a chance, hatred is so widespread and intense. People who should know told me that in Israel, Jordan, Lebanon, and Syria the people are behind the commandos. There are Christian elements in Lebanon who wish they'd go away. Signs scrawled on buildings in Beirut say, "Lebanon is for the Lebanese."

Gerard Chaliand, who wrote an excellent study for *Le Monde Diplomatique*, concludes with: "The strength of the Palestinian resistance lies in the fact that it enjoys the undivided support of the people of the Arab states." And that is what they call it, "The Resistance." While it has been divided and often inept, Chaliand believes that the Israelis have underestimated its strength, partly because they looked upon it simply from a military angle.

Although Fateh came into being among students and workers from the lower middle classes in the refugee camps of Gaza during the Israeli occupation after the 1956 war, progress for a decade was slow. The Palestine Liberation Organization was created in 1964 at the Arab summit meeting in Alexandria, at the time the Israelis set out to change the course of the tributaries of the Jordan River. The PLO, financed by the Arab states, organized an army as an integral part of the Arab armies. By June 1967 there were three Palestinian organizations, the PLO, Fateh, and a small group called The Heroes of the Return.

Fateh by-passed the red tape of the PLO and the Arab

governments and before the June war entered the struggle as an independent Palestinian guerilla organization. The Arab governments opposed Fateh and the Palestinian people generally remained uninterested. The refugees were still hoping that the UN would find a political solution or the Arab governments would do something towards their return. In the early part of 1967 guerilla operations were stepped up. The Israelis responded by hitting the Arab states so that they in turn would discipline the commandos.

Then came the June war. And since June 1967 the commando movement has grown into a serious threat and the Palestinians have emerged as a nation. They were given pride and some hope in their fighters – most of them young men who had grown up in the refugee camps.

By the end of June 1967 Fateh had met in conference and decided to continue the Resistance. In September operations were opened in Nablus, Ramallah, and Jerusalem, although there wasn't much popular support at first. Israel, with an expert intelligence set-up and harsh reprisals, forced the commandos to change their strategy and attack from across the frontiers rather than from within. This got them into trouble with the Arab governments, especially in Jordan whose armies could not stop the Israeli reprisals. New movements sprang up; some groups divided. Efforts were made to get them united. They finally came together in February 1969 – although different groups still have substantial autonomy.

The big change in commando fortunes and prestige had come March 21st, 1968, when the commandos stood fast for twelve hours and fought off – with the Jordanian army – a sizable Israeli attack on the town of Karameh, across the Jordan from Jericho. The Arabs reported they were attacked by four armoured columns, preceded by tanks and covered by air. When the Israelis withdrew they carried many dead and wounded and left a number of tanks and armoured cars behind.

Since then I have often driven by the ruined town of Karameh, built by the refugees and turned into a flourishing market town of about twenty-five thousand. It had begun as a tented refugee camp on the desert in 1952. Hard work and irrigation brought prosperity and development. When the new exodus of 1967 came, another twenty-five thousand refugees flooded in and thousands more camped round about. It was warmer there – and for most of the second-time losers it was just over the river from home in Jericho.

In the autumn of 1967, after severe storms had hit the tented camps in the hills of the north, thousands more headed to the Karameh area. Increasingly, or so it was rumoured, the fedayeen were moving in – and out, and over. Israel's defense minister warned, "There will be no room in the Jordan Valley for civilian life, families, children, cattle or cultivation" – as a threat to the commando attacks over the river.

Karameh got it first from the air. It was shelled on November 20th, and fourteen were killed. It was shelled again, twice in January and three times in February. The refugees packed up, against the advice of UNRWA officials, and headed back to the cold hills and snows of the north, where they had to suffer the weather but would be relatively free from the air. In three months over eighty had been killed and a hundred and forty wounded. UNRWA's John Defrates told me, "We told them not to go, but they have an instinct about these things. If they hadn't gone they would have been carved up."

For the Israelis the March 21st attack was probably not a serious thing; the set-back wasn't that bad. Certainly Karameh was left unoccupied and in ruins. But for the Palestinians, their boys had stood up to the superior Israelis, and the myth of Israel's military invincibility was destroyed. Since then you often see the slogan, "Remember Karameh." Chaliand says, "For the Arab states as well as for the Palestinian people, Karameh was an act of armed propaganda."

When I went back to the Middle East in September 1968 the most startling development during a year's absence was the stepped-up popularity and activities of the commandos. I had rarely seen the fedayeen before. They had kept away from the cities and covered their faces when their pictures were taken. But there they were, all over the streets of Amman. The PLO flag flew boldly from their headquarters in Beirut. Distinguished professors sat on their executive committees, students had Fateh posters on the walls of their halls and rooms. Almost

109

every day there was a report of a commando action in the press, invariably ending with the cliché, "All commandos returned safely to base."

At that time the chairman of their executive committee, Mr. Yehia Hammoudi, was quoted regularly in the papers. It was not difficult to get an appointment with him. He seemed a gracious and gentle man, fingering his prayer beads – a common custom in the Middle East – while he told me he hated violence and loved peace, but loved justice even more.

After Karameh the Palestinians began to talk about Palestinians – so did the rest of the world. The resistance movement began to consolidate itself, the recruits and the funds both began to roll in, and Israel began to notice – a little. The Western press made more of "the terrorists." In November there was a confrontation with Jordanian troops and King Hussein sent for Yasser Arafat to negotiate a settlement. Shortly after, the various Palestinian groups came together to set up an emergency council. Arafat of Fateh emerged as top man. He sold the two limousines which had been kept for the use of Mr. Hammoudi.

Arafat enunciated the principles first declared in 1958:

—revolutionary violence is the only way in which the fatherland can be liberated.
—this violence must be exercised by the mass of the people.
—the aim of this revolutionary violence is to liquidate the Zionist identity, in its political, economic, and military forms from all the occupied land of Palestine.
—revolutionary action must be independent of any control either by state or party.
—this action will be of long duration.
—the revolution is Palestinian in its origin and Arab in its extension.

The way it is usually expressed is, "We want Palestine to become a free democratic state where Christian, Moslem, and Jew can live side by side in peace and brotherhood with each man one vote."

I suppose I have heard it said and read it a thousand times:

110

"We have no quarrel with the Jews. Our quarrel is with Zionism. The Israeli-Zionist state is an imperialistic, racist and expansionist state."

The undergraduate son of one of my American friends in Beirut planned to spend his summer vacation 1970 in a Fateh camp. He was critical of Fateh though – "too conservative." And this is something one often hears from the young Palestinians of the New Left.

There are Marxists in Fateh, but not many and probably not in high places. The Popular Front, the PFLP, on the other hand, is Marxist. Fateh makes no attacks on non-military objectives – except four times, during four years, as very direct reprisals – but the Popular Front boasts of its attacks on civilian objectives and aircraft hi-jackings.

Despite the unified command of the PLO the numerous organizations still continue to act independently of one another in some things. On May 6th, 1970, after four months of negotiations, eleven major commando groups expressed their full allegiance to the PLO and it was announced that a central committee would be formed to replace the unified command. Within a few days the PFLP complained of not getting fair representation.

In Amman in mid-May I visited the public relations offices of three groups, including the Popular Front and Fateh, and heard explanations of where they were united and what the differences had been. The spokesmen at the Popular Front – attractive and, I suspect, intellectually superior persons – were obviously Marxist, and justified such actions as sabotage of El Al aircraft.

A Fateh spokesman told me:

"You know we are not opposed to the Jews, and to come right down to it our main fight isn't with Israel. Israel is just another nasty expression of Western imperialism by which we who live here are being exploited by those from abroad."

I asked him if the oil interests in the Gulf States, who, I suspect, gave some support and co-operation to Fateh, weren't also an expression of Western imperialism.

He said, "Yes, but we have our priorities, and Israel is first." Later I told that to a group of oil executives in Saudi Arabia. I thought it was rather amusing. But there wasn't a smile in the whole board-room.

I was taken by a young Fateh man to one of their camps near Amman, where three hundred boys aged ten to fourteen were being trained as young tiger cubs. Lads of eleven or twelve carrying automatic weapons stood guard. They shook my hand with the customary Arab "Welcome." They enter the fedayeen when they are fifteen.

The main show that day was a group of girl commandos – some of them schoolgirls, others office-workers – who were climbing a mountain carrying automatic weapons. Occasionally their instructor would fire above their heads. It all seemed like a lot of fun. Some of the girls wore semi-high heels; I saw boys helping them gallantly over the rocks, and then observed some television cameras grinding away. It was all for the benefit of Yugoslav TV. I don't think I would have been too frightened if I had been in Israel on the other side of the mountain; I would have been scared if I had been one of their instructors, with all those weapons banging around. I was told, though, that some of the Arab girls make tougher resistance fighters than the boys.

Mr. R. F. Owren, head of UNRWA in Amman, told me in early 1970, "The refugees are militant and armed to the teeth. We foreigners have a complete feeling of insecurity. We have two sets of authority. In practice I deal with the government – they go behind my back to clear with the fedayeen. Many of both the government and fedayeen people were trained by UNRWA, so we have good friends everywhere."

Fateh has set up its own hospitals, schools, camps, organizations for boys and girls, and in Amman a residential school for the daughters and sisters of "martyrs" – those who died or have been taken prisoner. About seven hundred Fateh had been killed since 1965, including those who fled in the June war – and those killed in fighting with the Jordanian and Lebanese armies. There was no such school for boys in 1970.

I found a great discrepancy between Fateh reports of numbers of Arabs in Israeli prisons and Israeli figures. Fateh says ten thousand; Israel says thirty-two hundred. The Red Cross and UN would support the Israeli figures. Fateh asks, "What happened to the others who did not return?"

"Jerusalem" is the name of the school and each small dormitory has a Palestinian name – and not for communities lost in 1967, but for Haifa, Jaffa, Acre, lost in 1947 and 1948. This is significant. There is no inclination in the Resistance to accept partition or the 1948 cease-fire lines, or the pre-1967 set-up.

The seventy-seven girls aged six to fourteen were being given full care – board, clothing, everything, including a training for the revolution and the post-revolution. "Everyone knows it will be a long time – so we are preparing for it," the principal said. The school administration has plans for a school of five hundred children of the revolution for both boys and girls.

I think "Jerusalem" was the neatest, cleanest, most orderly institution I saw in the Middle East. The curriculum is the same as the government's – although the teachers work for less pay. English is the second language being taught in the first grade. The children are taught Hebrew. "We should know the language of our present enemies, and that of our future friends and countrymen," I was told. I don't think this was just public relations. At the Conference of Christians in Beirut, Kamel Nassar, one of the senior spokesmen for the PLO, told the audience that when he visited a camp and asked the children about the Palestine problem he referred to "Jews." A child corrected him and said "Not the Jews – Zionists." When he asked one child why she was learning Hebrew, she said that some day they would be living together again with the Jewish people and they should know their language.

The school girls do their own housework. On each bed there was a doll – a blonde doll.

Fateh have their young people organized into "Young Tigers," and "Flowers of Fateh." They go to camps for training and some observers say these organizations form the most effective revolutionary movement among the people.

Abroad some have confused the Red Crescent with a revolutionary movement. The Red Crescent – similar to our Red Cross – has an active but different training programme in the

113

refugee camps. "Their job is to put kleenex in the camps, ours is to teach revolution," one Fateh girl told me. She added quickly though, "They teach the young girls how to take care of babies – and how to nurse the wounded."

Fateh has organized a network of public health installations and has one big hospital near Amman. The top doctor is a Palestinian and receives no salary. Nurses and doctors working for Fateh, like many of the young commandos, work out of a sense of dedication for little or no pay. Treatment and medicines in Fateh clinics and hospitals are free. One of the main sicknesses treated is malnutrition.

Along the Jordan front, underground medical clinics have been set up. They are even equipped with plasma; each commando carries a disc about his neck with his blood type on it.

In 1970 "making contact" was no problem. Any taxi-driver in Beirut, Amman, or Damascus would take you to Fateh.

I have a well-to-do Palestinian acquaintance in Beirut who has an excellent job with an American firm. He is a supporter of all good causes, something of a leader of the Palestinian community. In mid-1970 he was completely discouraged. "It's too late," he said.

And he explained. "I've tried to be a good citizen. I've worked hard – got through AUB, took graduate work in the US. I support several Palestinian organizations. I give to the commandos.

"But I wear a good suit, have nice ties (and in Beirut ties cost money), have a good job and home.

"A Palestinian friend came to me and said, 'We will need so much a month from now on.' I said, 'I just can't give that much.' He said, 'Now look, Abdul, you have a very good job and a big salary. You live in a lovely villa, and you have two cars. Your wife wears beautiful clothes and has two servants. The refugees are in tents. The young lads are ready to die. It will be so much.'

"I couldn't tell him," Abdul told me, "that I owe over a hundred thousand Lebanese lira on my house. That only one of the cars is mine – the little one. I use it and my house to entertain

114

my business people, I support my wife's family and some of my relatives or they might be in camps. I just couldn't do it. Well, he was my friend, and he understood. But next year or the year after one of the young Turks will take over and then he won't understand. I expect it will go communist. It's too late to stop it now. I see no hope."

I asked Fateh where they got their money. Palestinian workers are taxed from three to six per cent a month for the national fund. Arab states belonging to the Arab league contribute. (Some critics say that the reactionary states contribute to the commandos so they will remain preoccupied with the Palestine problem instead of trying to reform them.) There are private donors; organizations raise funds. Even the masses contribute their piastres.

"Some rich Arabs try to participate with small offerings," a PLO spokesman said. "I know one billionaire who wants to belong but gives us practically nothing."

A wealthy Libyan on the other hand looks after fifty daughters of the martyrs in the Jerusalem school.

In Israel I have asked what effect the commando movement was having upon them. One Israeli journalist told me in 1968, "They are a nuisance. They are young, inexperienced, untrained, and we're killing too many of them. Our intelligence is superb. We'll keep beating them with science."

An Israeli Air Force officer told me something the same: "We know everything they're up to. They start to 'sing' as soon as they see us boys."

An internationalist told me, "Israeli intelligence is good. And the Arabs talk too much. Also the Israelis have very effective ways of making them talk."

I have no way to estimate the effect on the Israelis. Sometimes I suspect that both Israelis and Arabs toughen under pressure.

But a Fateh spokesman said, "I don't speak for other groups. But we don't send untrained kids across. And we get our objectives. I was over the river last night and we got what we went after and we didn't get killed."

He told me that Fateh had had "sixteen hundred military operations in four years and lost three hundred and fifty men.

Algeria lost a million in seven years. Only four of our operations were against non-military objectives and they were direct reprisals for certain Israeli actions. After all, we count on future friendship with the Jewish community."

There is strong difference of opinion between Fateh and the Popular Front about this sort of thing. The PFLP believes attacks on El Al airplanes outside Israel are legitimate. The Zurich attack and the hi-jackings called attention to the problem. The PFLP argued it was "military."

The Fateh spokesman said:

"Guerilla warfare is a complete science. It's the war of the weak against the strong, and has always proved successful. We are certain – there is no doubt about it – we will liberate Palestine from Zionist occupation and turn it into a free democratic state for all the people. Remember this is not a struggle between Arab and Jew, it is a struggle between the oppressor and the oppressed."

The commandos are divided but not as divided as they were. The eleven or twelve guerilla organizations that existed before the September fighting in Jordan have been reduced to four. They maintain separate structures but in future, according to Yasser Arafat, they will "act jointly." Arafat, who condemned the hi-jackings as "an unnecessary cry in the night," came out on top as Supreme Commander, and claims that they "have more recruits than we can handle." There may be as many as fifty thousand fighters.

The Palestinian masses are still behind the commandos. When I asked Greek Orthodox Archbishop Deodorus of Amman about the fedayeen he said, "In Greece we build monuments to heroes. We should build monuments to the fedayeen for they are fighting for their country."

nineteen

The Arabs in Israel

WHEN THE STATE OF ISRAEL WAS FORMED IN 1948 ABOUT seven hundred and thirty thousand Arabs fled or were driven out; about a hundred and sixty-five thousand remained in Israel to become non-Jewish Israelis.

The Israeli propagandists have emphasized that such Arabs were citizens in the full sense of the word, with one exception: they could not serve, or were not called upon to serve, in the armed forces. The Arabs said, "They have made us second-class citizens in our own land." The Israelis argued that the Palestinians in Israel were better off financially than other Arabs and pointed out that some were members of the Knesset.

The Israel claims were generally echoed by tourists on their return from Holy Land pilgrimages. And when a curious tourist would ask questions of an Israeli guide about the obvious poverty of certain Arab communities it would usually be stressed that the Arabs were rather backward people and their poverty was their own fault. Israeli Arabs either did not talk to foreigners, or, for their own good reasons, gave approval to the Israeli policies when talking to strangers.

Little was actually known about such Arabs, even in the Arab world, until the publication in Haifa in 1966 of an astonishing book, *The Arabs in Israel,* written in Hebrew by a young Christian Arab lawyer named Sabri Jiryis. It very quickly disappeared. Arabs say it was "suppressed by the Israeli authorities." Copies were smuggled out of Israel in 1966 and translated first into Arabic and later into English and French.

I had often felt frustrated in Israel in my attempt to get at the true story of the Arabs. On the one hand I heard the most incredible stories of Israeli brutality and suppression from Christian workers who did not want to be quoted because they wished to continue working in Israel. I listened to glowing reports from Israelis. The Arabs in Israel I met were restrained in their comments.

When I read Jiryis' book in English in late 1968 I found it incredible. It did have the expected marks of a scholar and lawyer – numerous footnotes and references and legal language. Many of its most damning quotations were from the Israeli Hebrew press and from Israeli writers.

The *Guardian* (Dec. 12th, 1968) called it:

> "A scholarly work, it is a forthright and comprehensive study of the Arab minority in Israel. It contains the fullest and most vivid account yet published of the notorious Kafr Kassim affair in which Israeli soldiers systematically killed 49 Arab villagers as they returned home in ignorance of a curfew which had been imposed at short notice."

Actually the Kafr Kassim affair had received substantial publicity in the Israeli press. What few outside Israel knew until they read *The Arabs in Israel* was that the criminals served only a short time of their light sentences in prison or of the privileged positions later held by the murderers.

Lieutenant Joubrael Dahq, for example, the officer in charge, convicted of killing forty-three Arabs in one hour, was released after serving three and a half years of his prison sentence and was later engaged by the municipality of Rama as the "officer responsible for Arab affairs in the city." Israel has some distinguished precedents in elevating its most notorious Arab-killers to high office. The effect on Arabs is predictable.

I tried to find Sabri Jiryis in Israel but was unable to. Nor could I find an Arab who admitted knowing him, although a Baptist minister in Nazareth had seen him once and commented, "He is quite young. He is a graduate of Hebrew University, I believe."

I discovered, however, that Jiryis was well-known to Simha Flapan, the distinguished Jewish editor of the *New Outlook*, and an articulate spokesman for Israeli doves. He told me Jiryis was in prison, "but not for writing the book." He said he believed that he was going to leave Israel – that it was that or remain in jail. I understand Jiryis' trouble was about having made contact with persons outside the country considered to be enemies of Israel, and belonging to an organization within Israel that the Israelis declared illegal.

Flapan told me that, although he had two criticisms of the book, Jiryis' "facts and statistics are correct." He wrote like the lawyer he is. But Flapan said, "He was not fair to the many Jews who struggled to abolish discrimination against the Arabs, and the book is out of date. For there were many changes or improvements in 1965 and 1966, when the military administration in Israel ended." Flapan said that Jiryis deals with confiscation of land policies, which were "virtually stopped in 1965. Otherwise his facts and figures are correct."

I give some space to this, for I think the most helpful thing I can do for those who wish to understand is advise them to read Jiryis' book. You can get an English translation from the Institute for Palestine Studies in Beirut. Or you can get a short booklet of excerpts from the Fifth of June Society in Beirut, P.O. Box 7037.

Keep in mind what Flapan said. The facts are correct for the period Jiryis wrote about – up to 1965. But he does not give credit to liberal Jews who fought to have conditions changed. What is apparent is Israel got away with bloody murder for seventeen years while her propagandists lied to the world about the way the Arabs were being treated. And I can say, from first hand observation, that Israel is getting away with bloody murder in her newly acquired territories now.

Flapan told me that Jiryis had been imprisoned several times and that liberal Jews had helped him escape. In May 1970 they were negotiating for his release again, on condition he leave the country. He understood Jiryis had decided to go. Jiryis had turned down such invitations before.

When I first visited the Holy Land I took Israeli statements about their generous and democratic treatment of Arabs at face value. Several times I had long talks with Mr. Chaim Wardi, who was in charge of Christian Affairs for Israel. He was so well-informed I even assumed he was a Christian. He assured me that minorities in Israel were treated generously; that any dissatisfaction was that people just didn't like being a minority.

I asked Wardi in Jerusalem in 1957 how it was that the Jewish people had survived two thousand years of diaspora and persecution as a separate people. He answered with a smile, "Now I don't say this. But some people say 'It is because the Jews are God's chosen people.' "

Wardi attended the meetings of the World Council of Churches in New Delhi in 1961 and was busy behind the scenes helping the assembly prepare certain resolutions. To me at the time that seemed a good thing. Too many Christians had no knowledge of the persecution their fathers had inflicted on the Jewish people; no doubt there were hang-overs of those evil things present in the churches, and they should be expunged.

What seems apparent now is that the evils of past anti-Semitism in the churches or potential or latent anti-Semitism for the present or the future were not the chief concern of Israeli "ambassadors" to New Delhi and later at the Vatican. It was to persuade the ecclesiastical powers in the churches to accept and approve the State of Israel and its policies.

Another reason was suggested by Sabri Jiryis: "The Government of Israel has not hesitated to interfere in religious matters. It has succeeded because it has 'bought' the greater part of the religious leaders. . . . As far as Christians are concerned, Israel's interference has not been so great because the spiritual centres of these communities are in countries whose aid Israel still requires."

Jiryis concludes that the policy towards the Arabs in Israel "has been nothing more nor less than one aspect of the systematic Zionist policy followed vis-a-vis the Arabs in general — racial discrimination and repression."

Twice I have been in South Africa within a few days of being in Israel. I know no two countries in the world with so much in common, unless it is Rhodesia and Israel.

But the Israelis make the South African whites look like babes in the wood when it comes to practising apartheid and keeping another race in its place and misleading the world about it.

They have separation of the races on important things built in through culture, religion, and the rabbinical marriage laws. It has been more difficult to confiscate the Arab land and turn the people into hewers of wood and drawers of water.

Jiryis says that "all classes of the Arab population of Israel regard the Military Government as an institution which was established to achieve the following three fundamental objectives.

"1. To facilitate expropriation of Arab land by the authorities.

"2. To interfere in elections to the Knesset and municipal councils, in the interest of the Mapai Party and a group of hypocritical Arabs who do what they are told by this party.

"3. To prevent the formation of any Arab political movement which is either independent, or linked with any other political movement other than Mapai."

The success of their objectives is reflected in the changes in Nazareth.

In Israel, Nazareth is the main Arab town, with an Arab population of about thirty-two thousand. About fifty-five per cent are Moslem. Jewish Israelis have built a fine new municipality on the hills, with a population larger now than Nazareth itself had before 1948.

The first time I visited Nazareth was in 1957, and I was being shown about by a very fine and friendly New Zealand Jew who worked for the government, specializing in people like me. I remember the impression I got from him of backward Arabs crowded into backward places. With pride he showed me the beauties of Haifa and somehow I got the impression it had all been built by the Israelis since 1948. Arab Nazareth looked as though it had been that way from the beginning.

I didn't know then that the Nazareth Arab population, which prior to 1948 was largely Christian, had been doubled by an influx of Moslem farmers who had had their lands taken from them, or that the brand-new town being built on the suburban heights was erected on land taken by legal fiction from its original owners.

Even informed people had no idea of what Israel had done to Arab education until Jiryis told them that only a hundred and seventy-one Arab students out of a population of a quarter of a million were receiving a university education, while fourteen thousand Israeli Jews were in university. This for a Palestinian Arab people who had emphasized higher education and sent their graduates around the world! There were in 1969, for example, sixty thousand Arabs at university in Cairo. And Beirut in Lebanon has five universities overflowing with students.

Jiryis wrote:

"The intention of the Ministry of Education is to confuse the rising generation of Arabs in Israel. The history of the Arab people is falsified and represented as a series of revolutions, killings, feuds, plunderings and robberies, with the aim of belittling Arab achievements and triumphs through the centuries. Jewish history on the contrary is glorified and enriched.

"Even more outrageous are some of the questions in the secondary examinations. Questions connected with the Jews are extremely serious and to the point, and conform to the official party line of the Israeli government. The questions in Arab history, on the other hand, are mere riddles and emphasize the most trivial movements and feuds that have taken place in the Arab world, and the decline of the Arabs, ignoring all the great historical leaders who have embodied great qualities of the Arab nation. There is never a question about the prophet Mohammed, the Caliph Harun al-Rashid, the Omayyad Caliph Muawiya, or Saladin, who were some of the greatest men in Arab history . . . it is a nefarious plan to Judaize the rising generation of Arabs."

twenty

The Jews
in Arab Countries

"IT IS NOT THE ANTI-SEMITISM OF MEN: IT IS THE ANTI-Semitism of things," Vladimir Jabotinsky told the British House of Lords February 11th, 1937. "The cause of our suffering is the very fact of the Diaspora, the bedrock fact that we are everywhere a minority."

This comment was never more relevant or significant than to the Jewish minorities in the Arab world since 1948. The Arabs were not and are not anti-Semitic. They are Semites themselves, and cousins of the Jews. Objective historians have always reported on the historic tolerance of Jews and Arabs for each other. "It was not we who persecuted the Jews," Arabs will repeatedly tell their Western visitors. "It was the Christian West."

Yet look what has happened to Jews in Iraq, Egypt, Syria – most of the Arab world since 1948. The great, affluent, and respected Jewish communities of Alexandria, Cairo, and Baghdad have been destroyed. Over half a million Jews emigrated, some after persecution. Some left everything behind and arrived as refugees in Israel. Life for the most part is not good or secure for those who remained. In some cases they live in constant fear.

This was a by-product, probably unforseen by early Zionists, of the "return" and partition of Palestine. Jews left in the Arab world are looked upon by their former friends as potential enemies, possibly spies for Israel.

When anyone criticizes Israeli policies in respect to the

Palestine refugees he is open to attack on two points. First, for not remembering clearly what Hitler did, and secondly for not denouncing strongly what the Arabs have done to their Jewish minorities. When Iraqi Jews were hanged publicly in Baghdad because they were said to be "spies" for Israel there was outcry – as there needed to be – around the world. Christians did not rise up in protest that Christians too were hanged, or Presbyterians that one of the executed was a Presbyterian elder, believed, by local Christians and "foreign" missionaries and teachers, to have been completely innocent.

When I have written about Arab refugees I have been criticized – with some validity – for not having said something about the Jewish refugees.

When the United Nations voted overwhelmingly to investigate conditions among the native civilian population in the Israeli occupied territories of Palestine and Syria, Israel countered with demands that the UN investigate conditions among the Jewish minorities in Arab countries. To the unsophisticated this made a certain sense, and it was effective propaganda for Israel. For internationalists seeking to contribute to a settlement of a complex issue it was another one of those infuriating Israeli obstructions. Israel never did let the UN make its investigation and continues to violate major sections of the Geneva Convention in respect to the Arabs in occupied territories.

It would be good if conditions of Jewish minorities could be thoroughly examined by the UN or some appropriate organization. But it would be quite improper, as Israel well knew, for the proposal to investigate an occupied territory bounded by UN imposed cease-fire lines to be conditioned by the carrying out of another investigation to be conducted among citizens within the borders of a sovereign state. That may seem casuistry to the man in the street but it is very basic in international relations.

The outside world has a great abundance of misinformation and confusing information about the Arab refugees, and a small amount of information about Jewish refugees from Arab countries and about those still living in Arab countries.

One might divide the story of such Arab-Jews into three periods; prior to 1918, 1918 to 1948, and after 1948.

In Jerusalem I was once told by an elderly Jew, "We got along here fine until those Jews from Europe and North America came and started running things." Many times in the Middle East I have heard elderly Arabs rebuke young Palestinians for not clearly distinguishing between Jews and Zionists.

Terence Prittie, who is pro-Israeli, writes: "It says much for the mutual tolerance of individual Arabs and Jews that the two races mingled so well, comparatively speaking before 1948." He says also, "These Jews had been tolerated in Arab countries, but they had at the same time been forced into a position of inferiority. Emigration to Israel offered escape." So it depends a bit on whom you talk to. By and large they did better in the Arab world than anywhere else.

Jews have existed in the Arab world since earliest days. Some never did go back from Babylon when the faithful returned to rebuild the walls and restore the temple. During the fifteenth century persecutions under the Inquisition in Spain great numbers emigrated to North Africa and helped build up the great Jewish communities there. They enriched their new homes and often climbed to positions of eminence, and acquired great wealth. The Jewish imigrants from Arab countries today are called Sephardim, from the Hebrew word for Spain.

After the Balfour Declaration and the end of World War I, an intensive campaign was begun among Arab Jews by Zionists to join "The Return" to Palestine.

Prittie reports that: "About 170,000 Asian and Middle Eastern Jews entered Palestine, their guiding motive a spiritual attachment to the idea of a National Home." During those years they went freely for the most part, and managed usually to take what wealth they had with them.

As Theodor Herzl, the founder of modern Zionism, said in 1896:

"We must not imagine the departure of the Jews to be a sudden one. It will be gradual, continuous, and will cover many decades. The poorest will go first to cultivate the soil. In accordance with a preconceived plan they will construct roads, build-bridges, railways and telegraph installations; regulate rivers and build their own dwellings; their labour will create trade, trade will create markets and markets will attract new settlers, for every man will go voluntarily at his own expense and his own risk. . . . The emigrants standing lowest in the economic scale will be followed slowly by those of a higher grade. Those who at the moment are living in despair will go first. They will be led by the mediocre intellects which we produce so superabundantly and which are persecuted everywhere."

So the Zionists recruited the poor from Europe and from the Arab countries of North Africa and the Middle East. And it is difficult – in fact usually impossible – for the casual observer to tell the difference between a Jew and Arab in Palestine. The Sephardim are more like the Arabs – and in culture and in race more closely related than to the Western Jews – than they are like the Ashkenazim, the European Jew. (South African Jews, of whom there are many, North American and New Zealand Jews are Ashkenazim.) The Europeans run the country.

The Sephardim have been looked down upon by the Western Jews and treated as inferior and less cultured. They prefer that their sons and daughters not marry among them. Much is made of this "discrimination" by outsiders, including Jews from the US. Within Israel it is expected that the prejudice and discrimination will disappear in a matter of time. A new class of Jews, the Sabras, those born in Palestine or Israel, are fast moving up in the establishment. They tend to be more nationalistic than Zionist, more proud of being Israeli than of being Jews, and more intolerant of rich American Jewish tourists, whom they put up with for their money, than of "poor Jews" from Arab countries who have come to be Israelis.

While Israel has done a great job of providing for Jewish refugees, things have not all been milk and honey for the Jews who left Arab lands for Israel. In Beirut in 1968 a Jewish businessman, when asked about Israel, said. "If I left Lebanon I wouldn't go there. They are a bunch of socialists." One of the most commendable things about Israeli society is its egalitarianism.

This capitalist-socialist business has had a bearing on what happened in Arab countries; especially since 1948. **Prittie says:** "What happened after 1948 was different only in degree: the National Home had become a fact, and it acted as a magnet to Jews who would never have faced the challenge of emigration otherwise."

Actually what happened after 1948 was quite a bit different. Since then the Jew has come to be looked upon with suspicion everywhere throughout the Arab world. The public hangings of Jewish "spies" in Iraq was not a surprising thing given the present political conditions and traditions of that country. I was very seriously warned by Arabs not to go to Baghdad at that time myself. Americans were having a bad time. Christians were suspect. More than once in times of excitement in Arab countries I have been told by my Arab escort that members of the crowd wondered out loud whether I might be a "spy." It should be remembered that there has been popular gloating in Israel over the cleverness of their spies.

For Jews in parts of the Arab world these have been terrifying years. They have been in a position somewhat similar to Germans in the US and Canada during World War I, or Japanese on the West Coast during World War II, except that the Arabs tend to act on their suspicions with more speed and violence than North Americans.

Prittie says:

"In Iraq and Syria, Jews were attacked in the streets, reviled, and pillaged. They were no longer allowed to buy or sell property, their bank accounts were frozen, they were barred from schools, hospitals, and public institutions.

"In Egypt, hundreds of Jewish families were driven from their homes and their property was confiscated. There were bombing attacks on Jews, and after the Sinai campaign of 1956, so many restrictions were imposed on Egyptian Jews that normal existence, even on the humblest scale, was made impossible. In November of that year, an estimated 2,500 Jews were arrested and thrown into prisons and concentration camps. More than 20,000 more were ordered to leave the country – 4,000 of them within a period of seven days – and were permitted to take only one suit of clothing and a laughably small sum of pocket money with them; they had to sign statements that they would never return to Egypt and that they renounced all assets they may have possessed there. They donated these assets, under duress, to the Egyptian Government. Jewish lawyers were expelled from the bar, and Jewish physicians were ostracized by government order. Assets of Jewish banks, stores, and other firms were confiscated; they ran into hundreds of millions of dollars. The Great Synagogue in Cairo was taken over by the government and turned into a tourist show. Many other synagogues were closed down."

Not all went to Israel. Some were anti-Zionist and blamed the whole Zionist movement for their troubles. Numbers went to the North of France, to Italy, South America, and elsewhere.

Jewish critics of Zionism will point out that it wasn't just the Israeli development that brought on the pressures, especially in Egypt. Egyptian Christians haven't been too comfortable during the socialist revolution and many have emigrated. Capitalists generally, and the privileged communities of foreigners, disliked Nasser's nationalism, especially when it hit them in the pocket book. The Italians, Greeks, Lebanese, and Jews were not interested in "nationalization" and got out, if they could, with their wealth. The same was true for Syria. To listen to a group of well-to-do former Syrians in Lebanon talk you would get the impression that Syria and socialism were the real enemies of Arabs.

I have hestitated to write about these things for I have not the competence which I have tried to acquire on the Palestine refugees. The Israelis often speak of "the population exchange," and act as though it could have been a fine thing if only the Arabs had been willing to provide for their refugees the way the Israelis did for theirs.

But it is not the same. The Palestine refugees did not want to leave Palestine and the other Arabs did not want them to leave. The Israelis needed and worked hard to get the Jews in

Arab countries to immigrate. And when they arrived there were the vacated lands, shops, and houses of three quarters of a million Arabs to give them.

An objective summation is made by the Quakers in their 1970 report, *Search for Peace in the Middle East:*

"In some cases, Arab hostility to local Arabized Jews – in places like Yemen, Algeria, Morocco and Iraq – reached such intensity that Jewish property, jobs and lives were threatened. With mounting harassment, discrimination, and persecution, some of these Jews were stripped of their possessions and fled as true refugees to Israel. In other cases, Jews in Arab countries were subjected to intensive recruiting efforts by Israeli representatives. Some of those who chose to go to Israel voluntarily – and without having suffered particularly at the hands of their Arab neighbours – found themselves deprived of much or all of the property as they left for Israel. In other cases, some were able to make satisfactory arrangements to transfer their assets in some useful form.

"In any case, the government of Israel welcomed these newcomers, despite the fact that many of them were unbelievably distant in culture from the predominantly European Jews who created the state and still lead it. The Israelis showed both great humanitarian concern and high efficiency in incorporating these new settlers into the country.

"In any honest and comprehensive search for equity for all refugees, Arab and Jewish, efforts should be made to establish the claims of the Arabized Jews who moved to Israel against those governments in their former homelands where unfair seizures of property have occurred. True justice in the Middle East must be concerned with the rights of both Jews and Arabs wherever those rights have been violated. Appropriate international efforts should be made, as part of any eventual overall peace settlement, to deal with those claims and rights."

Although I have met and talked with Jews in the UAR, Lebanon, and Syria since 1964, I can't give much credit to what they told me. Not that I didn't believe them or consider them persons of integrity! But they were under duress and I was a stranger.

In Egypt the few who are there – not in jail – are looked upon as potential enemies, likely to be more loyal to Israel than to Cairo. Some make loud protestations against Zionism and Israel and they may be sincere. It is quite probable that left-wing students are sincerely anti-Zionist as left-wing Israeli-Jewish students are. Visitors are likely to be taken to the Jewish synagogue where a few worship and where it is certain the rabbi won't say anything against the regime. I asked a leading Cairo Christian if he had contact with a rabbi I had not and he said, "No, it wouldn't be safe." Safe for whom? I didn't ask. I suspect "discreet" would be a better word.

In Lebanon the Jewish community has always been treated correctly, and in time of internal strife – which is most of the time – effective efforts have been taken to protect their quarter from mob violence. But the very fact it is necessary to take such steps indicates there could be mob violence. At such times many foreigners are given special protection or evacuated. But Lebanese Jews are not foreigners.

The sad truth is that Jews see no future for their young people in Lebanon and they are quietly leaving. There are no problems for them; they are treated precisely like any other citizens, given their passports and permitted to take their wealth with them. It was predicted that in a few years just "old people will be left."

There are no Jews in Jordan. But there are about forty-five hundred in Syria, chiefly in Damascus and Aleppo, the two largest cities. In 1938 there were twenty-six thousand in Syria. It may be assumed that substantial numbers went to Israel.

In addition to the cloud of suspicion under which they live Jews in Syria suffer other severe handicaps. They are permitted to travel only four kilometres from the centre of Aleppo or Damascus. This keeps Aleppo Jews out of what I was told by a senior official of a UN agency is "the best restaurant," which is about a hundred yards beyond the four mile limit. "We are always watched," a Damascus Jew told me, and he took me to an inner sanctum and told me that in a low voice.

They can't emigrate or get their money out. That holds for other Syrians too. "Although if we could go we would have ways of getting our money out," a Jew in Syria told me. "We're good businessmen."

The businesses where the Jews were specialists in Syria have suffered with the drop in tourist trade. But much of what the Jewish people suffer is suffered by many other Syrians as their country passes through a socialist revolution. For those involved in and committed to the revolution, the sacrifices are not so keenly felt. For those who are unsympathetic, forced to the outside or unaccepted by their neighbours, life under the new Arab nationalist awakening can be harsh.

Another problem was explained to me at some length by a Syrian Jew of considerable standing: "We are short of marriageable men for our girls. They are doomed to die without having husbands or children."

I took some of these complaints to a friend who had a ranking position in the Syrian government, as I had taken some Palestinian complaints – informally, of course. He said he did not know of the "surveillance" of Jewish citizens and did not defend it. As for the shortage of husbands for the Jewish girls he was less sympathetic. "The young men went to Israel to fight against us. They can practise polygamy if they want to."

The one-time large Jewish community in Iraq has been reduced to about five thousand a UN official told me. They are thoroughly frightened – understandably.

The official added: "There was no anti-Semitism in the Arab world until 1948." They don't admit it is present now – and usually it isn't – but when the people who are suspected and made to suffer are Jews it is inevitable anti-Semitism will come.

This is another of the great tragedies of the whole struggle – a tragedy for which Israel and the rest of the world have some responsibility. In the final reckoning Jewish refugees must be compensated too.

It was not the anti-Semitism of men that made the Jews of

the Arab world into refugees. It was the anti-Semitism of things. The things were the Zionist movement, the partition of Palestine, the creation of Israel, and the events which followed. The things which have followed have been and continue to be a threat to every Arab from the Nile to the Euphrates and beyond. And innocent Jews among the threatened people become the objects of suspicion, wrath, anger, and violence from their former friends.

twenty-one

Oh Jerusalem!

IN ITS ATTEMPT TO BRING PEACE BY PARTITION TO PALESTINE in 1947 the UN declared that Jerusalem should be an international city governed by a Trusteeship Council on behalf of the UN. By so doing it recognized that Jerusalem, called a Holy City by Jews, Moslems, and Christians, has a very special place in the world.

Although Jerusalem was then small, the UN vision was large. The boundaries of the international city were to extend to Bethlehem in the south, Ein Karim in the west, Abu Dis on the east, and Shu'fat on the north.

The partition plan was unacceptable to the Palestinians and their Arab neighbours. They questioned and denied the right of the UN to impose such a settlement. In the war that followed there was bitter fighting in Jerusalem. When eventually a UN cease-fire was arranged East Jerusalem remained in Arab hands and the new Jewish city of West Jerusalem remained in Jewish hands. Barbed wire and smashed buildings separated the two. Most of the ancient churches, the mosques, and many of the synagogues and places holy to the Jews were left in East Jerusalem.

East Jerusalem and the West Bank were united with Trans-Jordan in the Hashemite Kingdom of Jordan. Israel proceeded to build up a modern city in West Jerusalem.

In the years that followed Christian pilgrims to the Holy Land discovered that only half of the places they wished to see were on one side or the other. They needed to make careful arrangements beforehand to cross through the Mandelbaum Gate at Jerusalem or they would go home disappointed.

Nazareth, Tiberias, and all of Galilee were in Israel. You could drive from Dan to Beersheba and stay in Israel. Bethlehem, Jericho, and half of Jerusalem were in Jordan. The traditional site of the Upper Room and Mount Zion were in Israeli Jerusalem; The Garden of Gethsemane, the Garden Tomb, the Mount of Olives, the Church of the Holy Sepulchre, and about forty other "holy places," were in Jordan-Jerusalem.

The Israelis were cut off from their Wailing Wall – the Israeli always refer to it as The Western Wall – which was all that had been left of their temple after it was destroyed in 70 AD. They lost the old Jewish quarter, many of their synagogues and cemeteries, and Hebrew University. The Palestinians lost over seventy per cent of their country, the homes and businesses of tens of thousands of their people, and all the Mediterranean coast except Gaza, a strip cut off from Jordan and attached to Egypt. And over half their people were homeless.

There were agreements in the cease-fire, such as the assurance that the Jews could visit the Wailing Wall, which were not kept. Jews from Israel were cut off from almost everything in the Arab world. Christians in Israel were permitted at certain times to cross into Jordan. Arrangements were made at Christmas for them to attend services in Bethlehem.

Once, crossing through the Mandelbaum Gate, I watched fascinated as two nuns in their habits drove a small English car past the barrier into the no-man's land. They jumped out of their little car, each with a license plate. One whipped around to the back, the other to the front, and attached their Jordanian plates, over the Israeli plates, hopped back into the car and in a few seconds were entering Jordan-Jerusalem.

In the June war of 1967 there was fierce fighting in Jerusalem, but the Arab sector fell quickly and Israel took over East Jerusalem along with the rest of the country. Immediately the Israelis began to demolish Arab homes in the old city to make way for the crowds of Jews and tourists to park their cars and buses and pray at the Wailing Wall. On June 28th, over the protestations of the Arabs and the rest of the world, Israel annexed East Jerusalem and the Arabs of East Jerusalem were given a new status that made them candidates for Israeli citizenship.

Israel speaks of this as "The Unification of Jerusalem." The Arabs call it "annexation." Officially, the Israeli Government *Gazette* called the act of June 28, 1967, by which this was done: "Declaration of the Extension of the Boundaries of the Jerusalem Municipal Corporation," and spoke of it as a merger carried out "for administrative purposes."

The UN General Assembly voted 99-0 to condemn the action. And the Security Council expressed its viewpoint with such strong language as "invalid," "deplores," "censures in the strongest terms," "condemns the failure of the State of Israel to comply with the afore-mentioned resolutions," and so on. Israel ignored the UN, and many of their friends in the outside world backed up Israel and denounced the UN.

In the Christian world conservative supporters of the Zionists were organized and statements issued promptly approving the Israeli action. For example the Executive Committee of the Scandinavian Evangelical Council met in early August and said succinctly: "According to Divine revelation in the Old Testament, the City of Jerusalem belongs to Israel and this includes all the historic places sacred to all religious groups." Now that's not the most respected ecclesiastical organization in Denmark nor is its theological viewpoint acceptable to enlightened churchmen, but it said in simpler, bolder terms, what more sophisticated and respected churchmen were saying. Even Reinhold Niebuhr signed a document published in the *New York Times* approving the "reunification of Jerusalem."

As late as September 15, 1969, the Security Council reiterated its position on Israel. The US has refused to acknowledge or accept the "unification." Secretary of State Rogers said December 9, 1969, "The US cannot accept unilateral actions by any party to decide the final status of the city."

Despite pressures from the Israelis, the influential UN member states kept their embassies and consulates at Tel Aviv and ignored Jerusalem as the capital of Israel.

However Jerusalem has pushed ahead. The annexation has

become another fait accompli. Repeated Israeli statements say the status of Jerusalem is not negotiable and Arab states say there can be no settlement under the present state of affairs. Many Arabs have been ousted, officials have been expelled, and an effective plan is operating to Judaize the whole city.

Although International Law expressly forbids the destruction of property in conquered or occupied territory, Israel has disregarded it. It would take many pages to list the homes destroyed, the properties expropriated, the Arabs arrested, intimidated, expelled, and other disturbing acts of the Israelis in Jerusalem.

Article forty-nine of the Geneva Convention forbids an occupying power to "deport or transport parts of its own civilian population into the territory it occupies." Israel, which has ignored this throughout the Occupied Territories, established in Jerusalem a "Bureau for Populating East Jerusalem," and announced, "ten thousand housing units will be constructed during the next four years providing accommodation for 40,000 additional inhabitants, 10,000 of them Arabs." That was in the *Jerusalem Post*, July 19th, 1968. Two years later great new apartment buildings were beginning to ring Jerusalem and stretch northwards toward Kalendia airport.

Christians slowly are leaving Jerusalem, tourists have decreased, and at Christmas and Easter the hotels and hostels that used to be crowded have lots of space. "There is no future here for our young people," parents will say and send them off to university or to find work somewhere else in the world.

At first both Arabs and Jews responded to the "unification" with interest if not enthusiasm. Jews from West Jerusalem and other parts of Israel flocked across to the East side and bought their souvenirs at deflated prices. Arabs from East Jerusalem went wide-eyed to the West, tremendously impressed by the big new modern city. They hunted up their old homes and speculated on the possibility that they would now receive compensation. There was, in the summer of 1967, considerable hope among the Arabs of East Jerusalem that life with the Israelis might become better. It didn't last long. It soon became obvious that Israel intended to Judaize the whole city. And it was soon obvious that the people were still not united.

On successive visits to the Holy City since 1967 I have found bitterness and hatred have grown. Though the walls are down there is very little mixing among the people of the two parts of the city. Arab Jerusalem before the June war had about seventy-five thousand inhabitants; Israeli Jerusalem had two hundred thousand. Many Arabs have since gone. Israel is in a recruitment drive to increase the Jewish population to five hundred thousand – and uses such slogans as "Have a second home in Jerusalem," and "Come and Build Jerusalem," and "Have your first child in Jerusalem." This, and the thousands of new flats being erected for Jews in East Jerusalem, is the handwriting on all the walls for the future. "It will remain a Jewish city and the capital of a Jewish state," almost all Israeli Jews are agreed.

It's possible, however, for tourists to come and go in Jerusalem and even to read the press and the booklets turned out in great numbers by the Israeli government and have no sense of what lies behind the facade of unity. Arabs are hesitant to express their convictions to strangers. Arab tourist guides are watched and listened to, and some have lost their jobs for being "political."

Some time ago an Israeli brochure enthusing over the glories of the re-united Jerusalem was sent to my desk. There was a picture of Mayor Teddy Kollek of United Jerusalem and the Arab mayor of East Jerusalem shaking hands. My enthusiasm was dulled, for that posed handshake was a long time ago. The last time I had seen mayor Rhoui el Khatib was in Amman; he had been expelled by the Israelis for his lack of co-operation. He told me that Israel was planning a belt of Jewish homes right across from East Jerusalem to Mount Scopus and the Mount of Olives. This would cut Arabs off from their adjoining suburbs. Later I was to see the houses going up. Mayor el Khatib was arrested at three o'clock in the morning and taken to Jericho, where he was asked to sign a statement saying he had been given due notice of the order to expel him for the preservation of Israel's security. He had never seen such an order.

There is on the western side of the Mount of Olives, high above Gethsemane and overlooking the old city, a small new church, Dominus Flevit, built in 1955 over the ruins of a fifth century church that marked the place where Jesus wept over the city. It seems a fitting place today. Mayor Kollek himself said in early 1968, "The Israeli administration in East Jerusalem has failed miserably. . . . The Arabs will not leave because they are attached just as we are attached. Making them inferior citizens will prove a costly policy." He was right, but his warning seemed to have no effect.

Is there any hope for future peace and justice in Jerusalem?

King Hussein has said that a shared Jerusalem is synonymous with peace – and he is sincere. He is also sincere and speaks for all Arabs when he says there cannot be peace if Israel hangs on to all of Jerusalem and denies Arabs their traditional rights.

Anwar Nuseibeh, one of Jerusalem's most distinguished Arabs – whose Moslem family has been the keeper of the keys of the Church of the Holy Sepulchre for six hundred years – says there are two simple requirements: the right of freedom for worship and access to the Holy Places for all people, and the democratic rights of the citizens of Jerusalem of all religions and races. Fortunately, in Israel there are numbers of young people, as Gavin Young has reported for the *London Observer*, September 1969, who want peace and justice for the Arab people in Jerusalem. One young Orthodox student told Young: "Real peace is the thing. I'd even give up the Wailing Wall for a genuine peace."

No responsible Arab wants to take away the Wailing Wall or put the barriers back up between East and West Jerusalem. But all Arabs deeply resent what has happened and is happening to them in Jerusalem. There has been no indication during the first three years of occupation that Israel has deviated one bit from her original determination to make Jerusalem – all of Jerusalem – the Jewish capital of a Jewish state and all that means for non-Jews in Jerusalem and for non-Jews whose homes are in Jerusalem but who are away and are denied return.

In 70 AD the Jewish temple was destroyed. In 135 AD many were massacred and the rest driven from the city. Nineteen hundred years later they came back; and one can understand Jewish enthusiasm and excitement over that return. One can also understand the bitterness of people who have been dislodged and expelled because they are not Jews.

Whenever I visit Jerusalem I go to the Garden Tomb. It is thought by some to be the very tomb of Joseph of Arimathaea, from which Jesus rose on the third day. It is a quiet and beautiful place, not unduly disturbed by the bus-loads of Christians who come from time to time to wander about, speaking in hushed voices.

There are two such tombs in Jerusalem. The other is within the Church of the Holy Sepulchre, believed to have been the site of Jesus' burial since ancient times. The first church was erected there by St. Helena, the mother of Constantine the Great, in 336 AD. The Garden Tomb, beneath a rock that looks like a skull, was discovered by Britain's General Gordon. Its claims to authenticity are not taken as seriously as that of the site accepted for nearly seventeen hundred years. An Arab Christian told me once: "When I go to the Holy Sepulchre, I believe that was the place. When I am in the Garden Tomb I feel it is the place."

It's difficult for me to feel the same about the Garden Tomb now, because of the tragedy that happened to its former keeper, S. J. Mattar, who was killed by an Israeli soldier in the Garden on June 6, 1967, and because of the strange teachings of the present keeper, the Rev. J. W. Van der Hoeven. Mr. Van der Hoeven must be an utter delight to the extreme rightists in Israel, who believe it is God's will that they annex what they have conquered and build up a Jewish majority on both sides of the Jordan River.

I had listened a few times to what seemed to me to be some strange comments from Mr. Van der Hoeven and members of his devoted staff. "We hope to see you next year – but Christ may have returned before then." And, "The Jews are coming to Christ."

One late afternoon I was sitting in the Garden. Mr. Van der Hoeven told me what he believes about Jerusalem and the whole sad problem.

"I believe the nation is ripe for a religious revival and the Jews will accept Christ in five years – all of Israel.

"They will be able to remain Jews in every sense if they accept Christ, although if they say 'Hallelujah' in a synagogue they will be thrown out.

"There will be a slaughter of Jews on the streets of New York and in San Francisco within five years. There is a big war of anti-Semitism coming. Holland is ready for the slaughter when the Russians come. I believe all Jews should come to Israel – this is their only way to escape."

Now it may seem unwise, even harmful, for me to report this sort of thing. But Mr. Van der Hoeven is a very attractive young man. The first thing he tells visitors is that his wife is an Arab – a Lebanese, and that his father is secretary to the Queen of Holland. And he meets and talks to thousands of visitors every year. They must be impressed.

"I like the American Christians best," he says, "they are so open and childlike. When Jews visit the Garden Tomb, do you know what they do? They take off their shoes. Do you know what the American Christians do? They stand in front of the tomb and have their pictures taken. I have only seen six people take their shoes off to enter the tomb. Four were Jews."

He told me that he always challenges Jewish tourists to immigrate to Israel. "It's the only way they will save themselves from the slaughter that is coming," Mr. Van der Hoeven declares fervidly. "It's the only way to express their Jewishness."

As for a peaceful settlement with the Arabs? The suggestion is anti-Semitic. "Some Jews who come here get so impatient with the arrogance of the Israelis and their bad manners and with things the Israelis are doing they become positively anti-Semitic," he said. "I had to straighten an anti-Semitic rabbi out the other day. He was from the States. They're as bad as the Arabs. That's why other people criticize Israel – they're anti-Semitic."

As for the Israelis withdrawing from the territory occupied in the June war: "That's a laugh. Why should they? Is America going to give what she took back to the Indians? Why shouldn't the Israelis take the south of Lebanon too? They have had provocation enough." I asked about Lebanon, for that day the UN had censured Israel for an attack on Southern Lebanon. I gathered he thought the UN was a big joke too.

Van der Hoeven thinks those of us who think differently than he does haven't understood our Bible or what God is like.

"I'm amazed at these naive Christians who can read their Old Testaments and see what God is like and then be upset at the same God when he sends a little refugee woman with a baby in her arms across the River Jordan." He told me he was angry that when we wrote about refugees we always just talked about the Palestinians and didn't say it was a "population exchange," and that the Arabs had expelled six hundred thousand Jews who came to Palestine.

Mr. Van der Hoeven has much of this and much more on a record one may purchase at the Garden Tomb. It is one of the strangest mixtures of premillenialist anti-communist nonsense I have ever heard. In the New Jerusalem this is what one now gets in that quiet spot which has been and continues to be a chosen place for so many of what the keeper calls "simple child-like Christians." His comments are a travesty of the Gospel.

Weary of it all, I changed the subject to ask about his opinion of the authenticity of the Garden Tomb. He smiled with pleasure: "The Israelis are excavating. They will discover things that will prove the Church of the Holy Sepulchre was not the real site. It's a joke anyway that the crucifixion and resurrection would both take place so close to each other they could build one church over both. When the Jews" – and he often speaks of Jews rather than Israelis – "find where the old walls really were and when the credibility of the Church of the Holy Sepulchre is decreased, the credibility of the Garden Tomb will be increased." And that, I was made to feel, would be good for business and worth looking forward to.

One of the shocking things is that this sort of propaganda is permitted on what is, for many Christians, one of the most sacred sites in the world. I don't know who is responsible for the operation of the Garden Tomb, but local leaders of the Jerusulem Church seemed unconcerned.

Those who listen to and accept this from a Christian, on top of the Israeli propaganda, may wonder: Why all the fuss about Jerusalem? In one of the beautiful booklets given to tourists there is a final paragraph about the situation by Aba Eban:

141

"Where there was hostile separation, there is now constructive civic union. Where there was once an assertion of exclusive and unilateral control over the Holy Places, exercised in sacrilegious discrimination, there is now willingness to work out arrangements with the world's religious bodies – Christian, Moslem and Jewish – which will ensure the universal religious character of the Holy Places. The Government of Israel is confident that world opinion will welcome the new prospect of seeing this ancient and historic metropolis thrive in unity, peace and spiritual elevation."

This was in 1967 when the UN condemned Israel 99-0 for her actions in Jerusalem.

And that reminds me of a statement quoted by General Burns, attributed to Mr. Ben Gurion when he was Prime Minister:

". . . the function of the Ministry of Foreign Affairs is to justify in the eyes of the world, the actions of the Israeli Defense Forces."

twenty-two

Dissidents in Israel

ONE OF THE FEW BASES FOR HOPE IN AN INCREASINGLY HOPE-
less Middle East situation is the rising tide of outspoken criticism by Israelis of their government's policies. It comes chiefly
from intellectuals and from young people. How numerous the
critics are and how influential their opposition is I am not able
to judge. Certainly in the early summer of 1970 it had grown.

Although in this book I have been largely critical of Israelis,
there is much, very much, to be said for Israel. Fantastic
things have been done in a short time under difficult conditions.

One of the best things you can say is there is lots of talk.
You don't get jailed for talking or writing letters to the editor
or even publishing a book. Jiryis' book was written in Hebrew
and published and sold in Israel. It disappeared from the
shelves and Jiryis went to jail, but not for writing the book.

The Israeli Jews debate their problems freely and passion-
ately. The Arabs are naturally more inhibited and they are
careful what they write, but the thirty-two hundred Arabs in
Israeli prisons aren't there for criticizing Israel.

The two most articulate critics of Israeli policy best known
to the outside world are, I suppose, Uri Avnery and Simha
Flapan. Avnery is publisher of the *World*, Israel's largest
weekly. Flapan is editor of the intellectual monthly *New Outlook*. Avnery is head of his own small party and an elected
member in the Knesset. Flapan is a socialist, pacifist, and
Zionist – "quite a combination I know," he said to me. He

143

entered politics in 1948 and says he regrets it to this day. He served as secretary of the Mapam (labour party) and then as director of the Arab affairs department of Mapam. He spent three years in France trying to bring about an Israeli-Arab dialogue.

Avnery's book *The Arabs and Israel* calls for a de-Zionization of the Israeli state. He is considered Israel's number one maverick and champion of Arab rights and some Israeli young people work their hearts out for him at election time. He would turn Israel into a secular, pluralist, and multi-national state and would abolish the Law of Return, which gives every Jew the right to enter Israel and become a citizen. He says that Zionism's pan-Judaism keeps alive among Arabs "the myth of an Israel submerged by millions of immigrants who, finding no place to settle, would oblige the government to expand the country by force of arms."

I. F. Stone examines Avnery's writings in *Les Temps Modernes* and finds Avnery just another Jewish nationalist beneath it all. When I quote Avnery in Canada, Zionist rabbis scoff, "He is a pornographer." In Amman a spokesman for the PLO told me that Avnery was just another Zionist who, having discovered he couldn't fight in the trenches any longer, had changed his tactics. However Avnery is respected and followed with hope by many young Jewish Israelis, and gives encouragement to the Palestinians that at least there are friends in Israel who see their point of view.

In May 1970, in a periodic spasm of "trying to be fair" to the Israelis, I asked the Israeli Consul in Toronto if he would write a piece for the *Observer*, presenting the Israeli point of view. I suggested the hope that he would keep personalities out of it and instead of his customary attack on Canadians such as me, who had made criticisms of Israel, would do a straightforward piece.

He agreed but indicated that it would not be politic for him to appear in an issue that might carry certain critics of Israel. So what else did I propose for that issue? I answered that I though I might have this and that, and maybe a piece from Simha Flapan and perhaps a statement from Avnery, so my readers could see there were different viewpoints among the Israelis.

He said emotionally that he would have to refuse to appear in an issue that carried Avnery but "Simha Flapan is a distinguished Israeli and I would be pleased to appear in the same issue as he." So I agreed. Later, in Tel Aviv, I asked Flapan why the Consul would make this distinction.

He said it was because "I am trying to get the government to alter its policies; Avnery is in opposition to the government." Flapan is a flexible Zionist. Avnery wants de-Zionization.

Flapan calls himself a dove and he expressed his position and that of the Israeli doves in a letter to the *New York Times*, March 15, 1970:

"They demand a clear and unequivocal acceptance by Israel of the Security Council resolution [November 1967] viewed and implemented as an indivisible whole; they oppose the insistence on 'direct negotiations,' not because this is morally wrong but because it is unrealistic. They recognize the existence of the Palestinian people and their right to self-determination, and they demand immediate unilateral steps by Israel for rehabilitation of the Palestinian refugees."

I saw Flapan in his cluttered Tel Aviv office about ten weeks later. During the interval Israel had been going through the "Goldmann Affair." Nahum Goldmann, former head of the World Zionist Organization and now head of the World Jewish Congress, had written an article called "The Future of Israel" for *Foreign Affairs*, published in April 1970. He recognized that things had not gone right for Israel and proposed that Israel should be neutralized. "I am coming to the conclusion," he wrote, "that Israel cannot be one of more than a hundred so-called sovereign national states as they exist today and that instead of relying primarily and exclusively on its military and political strength it should not merely be accepted but guaranteed, de jure and de facto, by all the peoples of the world including the Arabs, and put under the permanent protection of mankind." Goldmann offered to go to see Nasser and apparently there had been some preparations made before he made the offer.

The Israeli government said no.

And then Israel had the "Goldmann Affair," and such moderates as Flapan were encouraged.

"Time is running out," he told me. "I don't know in whose favour. I still believe it is not too late. But in another half year the Arabs and Israelis won't be able to decide anything. It will be the USSR and the USA."

He said that the "Goldmann Affair" proved that many more people in Israel were in favour of flexibility than had been assumed. The young people were interested in a political solution. There was an obvious rift between the people and the government. The people no longer believe there is no other way. It became obvious that the majority of the people favoured a political settlement. The largest daily paper in Israel swung from support to criticism of the government's foreign policy. And Mapam was demanding the exclusion of the right wing party from the government. The right wingers favoured the "larger Israel" policies.

Flapan told me it had been a serious mistake not to allow the refugees to return in 1967.

In Israel there were numerous protests against repression and annexation. The Tel Aviv "Area Council for Peace and Security – Against Annexation" adopted a resolution as long ago as August 1, 1968, urging the people to support the following and other demands:

> "The government should once more unambiguously declare that Israel is not seeking territorial aggrandisement . . . should put an end to Jewish settlement in occupied areas . . . should refrain from expropriating lands . . . should make public a plan for the rehabilitation of the Arab refugees . . . action likely to increase the number of refugees should be avoided. . . ."

The Mapam and others have demanded that the blowing up of Arab homes should cease.

Mr. Flapan gave me a 285-page book, *To Make War or*

to Make Peace, which was a special issue of *New Outlook* reporting the proceedings and speeches of distinguished Israelis, some Arabs, and other guests at a 1969 symposium in Israel on the subject. I was surprised by the out-spokenness of so many of the participants.

For example, Professor Shimon Shamir, head of the Middle East department at Tel Aviv University, blasted the Prime Minister of Israel, rebuked the foreign minister, criticized the government, and boldly laid down steps by which Israel might right some of the wrongs. He excused the Palestinians for not being enthusiastic about proposals for a programme made by the Israeli government which "was neither sincere nor showed serious intentions on the part of the Israeli government to implement."

He charged that Israel's failure had destroyed credibility with the Palestinians and ended: "We have to begin to liquidate the Israeli-Arab conflict in the place where the conflict began, in our relations with the Palestinian society."

Professor Jehoshua Arieli of the Hebrew University: ". . . we have been deeply guilty, or, worse than that, criminally stupid for not having tried to solve the problem of the Palestinian refugees alone. . . ." The professor goes on to blame the Arab governments, but I wondered what would be said of someone in a Canadian Church who charged the Israelis with being "criminally stupid." It is what a good many wise Israelis are saying. Unfortunately they are running the universities, not the government.

Dr. Nahum Goldmann wrote to the symposium: "the more nationlistic elements dominated the Israeli press creating a distorted image of Israel and causing the country and the people great harm. It is my conviction that the time has come for those groups and personalities to make their voices heard who realize that understanding with the Arab world is the Number One problem of Israel's future."

But a wistful note came at the end under a section titled "Why We Didn't Come." Two prominent Arabs, Anwar Nuseibeh and Dr. Aziz Shedade, had been invited but sent regrets.

Nuseibeh, one of Palestine's most distinguished citizens,

and friend of Flapan's and occasional contributor to the *New Outlook*, wrote from Jerusalem:

"We deeply regret our failure to participate, however very inadequately, in this distinguished forum. The mounting spiral of violence and counter-violence culminating in mass arrests, destruction of property and the death under questionable circumstances of an Arab suspect during Israeli police investigation leaves us to doubt the value, or even relevance of whatever little contribution we can make toward better Jewish-Arab understanding. Yet we refuse to relinquish our firm conviction in the need for such an understanding any more than we can relinquish our faith in the normal process of democracy or the moral validity of public opinion. To us violence is not a satisfactory substitute for reason. However this sentiment we feel must be reciprocated by others.

" . . . It is conceded all around, we think, that Israel can make war successfully, but it is important that it demonstrate a like ability to make peace as well. . . ."

Dr. Shedade wrote:

"I was looking forward with a mixture of hope and apprehension to this important symposium on Israel-Arab peace. I wanted to tell you that peace is possible if there is mutual and unrestricted recognition of the rights of both people to build a homeland in this country. . . . I also believe that peace and reconciliation are possible if Israel abandons all expansionist views and the Arabs abandon the idea of the destruction of Israel. However I could not attend this meeting because of the worsening conditions of my people in occupied territories lately. I am afraid that if the situation continues the voices of peace will be stifled and the seed of peace which was planted by people of goodwill from both nations may be destroyed. . . ."

In Israel there are Jewish young people of the New Left

who call the Flapans and the restrained socialists, academics, and reconcilers of their ilk – "old hypocrites." How many or how important they are, I don't know. But their voices are heard abroad and their friends are working with Arab friends in the universities of Europe and America. They are Marxists and they identify closely with the aspirations of the extreme left among the Palestinian fedayeen.

One of the youth organizations is "Matzpen." It has a monthly paper – the word means compass – with a circulation of a few thousand. It is not a political party but an Israeli socialist organization with student and worker members, Arab and Jew. Some of the members are in prison or under house arrest. A spokesman said, "Generally speaking, they are the Arab comrades." They too are for the de-Zionization of Palestine. "This country belongs to its inhabitants, Arab Palestinians and Israeli Jews. They must fight against Zionism for a common future. . . . Obviously this will not happen without a revolutionary uprising," a Jewish member says.

One of the comrades, Dr. Machovar, wrote in *Le Monde*: "The creation of a binational state, or simply of one common state, where all ethnic and religious discrimination would be banned whoever was in the majority, is the only goal which corresponds to the needs of a durable peace and progress in the area."

I heard precisely the same thing from spokesmen for the PLO and the Popular Front in Beirut and Amman. The two groups have another thing in common – they are young.

twenty-three

Israel
and International Law

IT IS OFTEN SAID WITH SOME PRIDE THAT ISRAEL WAS THE creation of the United Nations. It was the UN decision to partition Palestine of November 29th, 1947, that made the State of Israel possible. Thirty-three UN states voted for the partition; thirteen were opposed, and ten, including the United Kingdom, abstained. The majority was secured after remarkable lobbying and last minute pressure on doubtful states. This UN decision is referred to by many supporters of Israeli policies as the ultimate authority for Israel to proceed to declare itself a State.

It seems ironic that later unanimous decisions by the UN have been ignored. The General Assembly vote of 99-0 condemning the annexation of East Jerusalem and calling on Israel to "rescind all measures taken, and to desist forthwith from taking any action that would alter the state of Jerusalem," on July 4th, 1967, was flouted. In late 1970 Israel is continuing to erect high rise apartments on Mount Scopus in East Jerusalem.

Ambassador Michael Comay and other Israeli officials told me that there was no way by which Israel would give up any portion of Jerusalem. Israel has repeatedly declared she would not withdraw from Jerusalem. But the November 22nd, 1967, Security Council resolution includes as a condition of settlement the withdrawal of Israel from occupied territories. This was adopted 15-0.

In some ways Israel's violations of the Fourth Geneva Convention for the protection of civilian persons are even more serious. It seems a strange paradox that Israel would refuse to abide by the conventions of international laws which were written as a direct result of the Nazi treatment of the Jews and other innocent people during World War II.

Following that war the Geneva Convention "relative to the protection of civilian persons in time of war" was drawn up, and signed by most civilized nations, including Israel. The world vividly remembered the awful abuses carried out by both the Nazis in Germany and the Japanese in Asia. They were determined that such abuses would never occur again.

Four Conventions were approved: the first three concerned the protection of sick and wounded armed forces in the field, armed and shipwrecked naval forces, and the treatment of prisoners of war. Each of the Conventions was consistent with the Universal Declaration of Human Rights of 1948. Israel signed the Conventions and has observed the first three. Whenever it has been to Israel's interest to invoke the charter of the United Nations, or seek the security of international law, she has done so. When it has been in her interest to ignore the UN or flout the Charter, she has also done so – without hesitation and, so far, with impunity.

The blowing up of houses, the destruction of property, the individual or mass transfer of populations from occupied territory, are all expressly forbidden. Collective punishments and reprisals are forbidden. Yet books could be filled — in fact books are being filled — with accounts of incidents and records of Israeli breaches of the Convention.

For example, Article thirty-three states: "No protected person may be punished for an offense he or she has not personally committed. Collective penalties and likewise all measures of intimidation or of terrorism are prohibited. Reprisals against protected persons and their property are prohibited."

I do not like to refer in any way to Israeli treatment of the Arabs as "Nazi," but the parallels are so numerous and so similar that Arabs speak of Nazi tactics and practices frequently. The Israelis have relied upon a systematic destruction of homes and villages to suppress resistance.

Article fifty-three of the Fourth Convention says: "Any

151

destruction by the occupying power of real or personal property belonging individually or collectively to private persons or to the State or to other public authorities or to social or co-operative organizations is prohibited except where such destruction is rendered absolutely necessary for military purposes."

On a main street in Gaza eight houses were blown up after a Jewish merchant was killed. There was no apparent attempt to apprehend the murderer. Reprisals were simply taken against the owners of the nearest homes. One of the owners was in Kuwait, another was an elderly woman. One can go down the list of the eight and the indications are that the victims were all innocent. This is typical. By mid-1970 something in excess of eight hundred homes had been individually destroyed and another seven thousand Arab homes had been brought down by the Israelis in one way or another. Red Cross observers told me that the Israelis have followed six different methods of destroying Arab homes, four of which blatantly contravene Article fifty-three. Two of the methods might be interpreted as militarily excusable.

The first contravention is the classical destruction of an Arab home as a punishment or reprisal. Israeli authorities, acting on information or suspicion known only to themselves, move in, order the householders out, dynamite the home, and leave, forbidding the owner to rebuild.

Then there are collective reprisals, such as the destruction of the eight homes in Gaza. In the village of Hebron eighty such homes were destroyed. Ten Arab villages were razed and all homes destroyed — some, apparently as reprisals, some, according to the Israelis, for security reasons. One village, from which apparently Fateh could not be driven, was sprayed with liquid fuel and destroyed. This, according to the Red Cross and international observers, might be exempted from the general condemnation for military reasons under Article fifty-three.

When East Jerusalem was taken, the Israeli authorities destroyed about one hundred Arab homes near the Wailing Wall to provide easy access for Jewish worshippers and a parking lot for tourists. In the Golan Heights and in some other areas unoccupied Arab homes have been crumbling down and indications are the crumbling has had considerable assistance from Israeli troops. This, too, may not contravene the Geneva Convention.

There are numerous types of punishment, which have been imposed by the Israelis on the civilian population, which are considered to be both collective punishments and reprisals. The Commissioner-General of UNRWA, in reference to Gaza, wrote: "The succession of incidents and security measures such as curfews, interrogations, detentions and, on some occasions, the demolition of houses which followed" were used to suppress, intimidate, and punish.

On November 2nd, 1968, many of the Arab shopkeepers in Occupied Jerusalem did not open their shops. The Israeli authorities regarded this as a strike and promptly confiscated fifteen shops owned by prominent Arabs. The *New York Times* described the matter: "Israeli officials confiscated fifteen Arab-owned shops in East Jerusalem today for what they described as security reasons.

"The seizures were said by the Israelis to have been necessary for billeting Israeli policemen who needed the strategic locations to maintain public order. The action was announced a few hours after the start of a strike by East Jerusalem shopkeepers and is regarded by many as an Israeli response."

Mr. W. T. Mallison, Jr., Professor of Law at George Washington University and an expert in international law commented on this: "The action taken was clearly a reprisal directed at civilians and their property and therefore a violation of Article thirty-three."

One of the most blatant abuses has been the transfer and deportation of civilian population. Article forty-nine forbids this: "Individual or mass forcible transfers as well as deportations of protected persons from occupied territory to the territory of the occupying power or to that of any other country occupied or not are prohibited, regardless of their motive. The occupying power shall not deport or transfer a part of its own civilian population into the territory it occupies."

153

These prohibitions were most definitely designed to make illegal the well-known Nazi practices of removing the "inferior" civilian population of an occupied territory to make room for the "superior" German population.

Mallison points out, "it should be noticed that the quoted provisions of Article forty-nine are flat prohibitions which are subject to no exception of any kind." He goes on to say, "the individuals who are deported by the government of Israel in violation of the Convention are frequently leaders and notables. For example, a large number of the leading citizens of Jerusalem, Jordan, including its mayor, have been deported. The apparent purpose is to eliminate Arab leadership in the occupied territories and to make it more difficult for the remaining civilian population to protest against the oppressive and illegal measures to which they are subjected. Among the individual deportees are substantial numbers of school teachers. In Gaza, for example, the Commissioner-General of UNRWA has reported that forty-eight teachers have been deported."

After getting rid of the civilian population, Israel has brought in its own settlers to the areas from which the Arabs have been expelled. In order to provide a technicality for justifying such movements, Israel has called the new settlements military settlements. They have established about fifteen settlements in the Golan Heights, and even one on the bank of the Dead Sea at Qumran.

Israel has established kibbutzim in Egypt's Sinai, where their technicians are drilling for and pumping oil, and where an important tourist business is being developed. But the most flagrant breach of all is in East Jerusalem itself. By annexing instead of occupying East Jerusalem, Israel sought to provide a technicality for justifying its movement there and its treatment of the Arab citizens. To the International Red Cross and, for that matter, to the whole world, this was completely unacceptable.

Article four states that: "Those who at a given moment and in any manner whatsoever find themselves in case of a conflict or occupying power of which they are not nationals are among the protected persons."

In April 1970, the Israelis cordoned off a seven hundred

and forty acre area at Hebron "for security reasons." The Arabs protested – so did some Israelis – predicting that this would be another movement of Zionists into occupied territory. The Israeli military claimed it was for military purposes.

On May 21st 1970, the *Jerusalem Post* carried the following news item:

"JEWISH HOMES IN HEBRON TO GO UP IN 3 MONTHS"

"Israeli Deputy Premier Yigal Allon has said the first homes for Jewish families in Hebron on the occupied Jordan West Bank will go up in three months.

"Allon told members of the ruling labor alignment Tuesday that 250 housing units would be ready in Hebron – where the question of Jewish settlement has created considerable tension – before the end of 1971.

"He said the Israeli cabinet also had plans for the building of new homes for the present group of 140 Jewish settlers already established in the town.

"Plans to build an additional large Jewish urban quarter in the town, which has a population of some 40,000 Arabs, were still open, he added.

"Last month, Israeli military authorities cordoned off a 740-acre area near the town's military government for security reasons amid Arab charges that the area would be used to settle Jewish families."

Within Israel itself there is considerable embarrassment and protest against such flagrant violation of the Geneva Convention. Mr. Arie Eliav, secretary-general of Israel's ruling labour party, Simha Flapan, and Meir Yaari, Mapam's general secretary, all protest the reprisals, the proposed annexations, and destruction of Arab homes. And in an article in *Le Monde*, February 11th, 1970, Yaari outlined an eight point peace plan that began with this:

"Israel should put an immediate and unconditional end to the establishment of kibbutzim and civilian Jewish villages in the occupied territory."

Arabs add up these things and cannot help but be impressed

155

more with what Deputy Premier Allon says he is going to do and then does, than by what more flexible labour leaders say should be done.

Articles seventy-nine to one hundred and thirty-five provide a detailed code of conduct for the occupying power in its treatment of civilians who are interned. These articles were drawn up against the background of the infamous Nazi concentration camps, but often in Israel the treatment accorded internees seems more like what happened in some of the concentration camps than like what the Geneva diplomats hoped.

The Israeli government denies many of the charges made by both impartial observers and by the Arabs. However, the Tel Aviv government has refused to permit an impartial enquiry.

On March 3rd, 1969, the UN Human Rights Commission in Geneva adopted a resolution denouncing the Israeli rule in the Occupied Territories and established a special working group to investigate the alleged Israeli violations of the Civilians Convention. The government of Israel immediately announced that it would not co-operate with the UN group and their action was sufficient to frustrate any attempt at such an investigation. The numerous reports have been studied, of course, and the documentation is piling up.

It seems to me that if any other nation in the civilized world treated its occupants in this way, the whole world would be informed. Mr. Mallison says: "To the extent that the government of Israel fails to co-operate with authorized UN fact-finding agencies, its refusal justifies the invocation of further sanctions." He says it is essential that the world public opinion be completely informed of the facts of the situation and the need for particular sanctions.

twenty-four

Israel's Prisons Are Crammed

AFTER THREE YEARS' ADMINISTRATION OF TERRITORIES TAKEN from the Arabs in 1967, Israel's prisons are crammed.

There is a constant flow in and out of prison – the arrest in the night, the confinement without charge, trial or sentence without communication with a lawyer or family, are common. The beatings, psychological pressures to exact information, all the features for which the political prison in time of war is noted, are said to happen in Israeli prisons. Internationalists such as the Red Cross are in no position to deny it. It is assumed the Arabs exaggerate and the Israelis suppress. The United Nations has been refused permission to investigate. Israel even denies there is an occupation.

The Red Cross will say that the prison authorities do their best with overlapping, crowding, and a shortage of staff. But there is an urgent need for more jails and many of the problems derive from the crowding and lack of staff.

The Red Cross admits that no one really knows what is happening. The Red Cross was trying in mid-1970 to work out a system by which they could see everyone arrested and held within a month. But humanitarianism and the urgent desire to get information collide. The Red Cross visits each prison once a month and tries to see everyone without a witness. But they are not permitted to talk to anyone under active interrogation. So the following month they try to see those they didn't see the last time. The Red Cross is seeing ninety-three per cent of the prisoners. But this means that the really hot customers may be kept from seeing anyone for a very long time – some can be kept in solitary confinement.

The army issues strict orders forbidding the use of physical force but there is considerable rough handling of prisoners when they are first taken. The psychological pressures applied are brilliant – the screams in the next cell and the sounds of beating, the putting of strict Moslem women in with prostitutes, the use of the dogs which the Arab hates and fears. The documentation of brutality is increasing and it can't all be wrong. Many arrested are young dissidents.

It is impossible to have a state of war and occupation and resistance without incidents of brutality. And it is probably inevitable that in order to establish a military control over a defeated people some politicians will have to be expelled or detained. "The scandal is not in administration detention but in the conditions under which they are detained," a Red Cross staffer told me.

In Gaza the Israelis introduced a new wrinkle that, for some reason, has been overlooked by the outside world. In order to keep local leaders quiet and inactive they are arrested and banished to the desert. They are usually attached to an Israeli army unit in isolated places but they have no contact with army personnel.

The first to be banished were three prominent citizens of Gaza in 1969; they were left three months. "The desert completely undermines a man's morale," I was told. When I was in Gaza in May 1970, six notables were still in the desert after five months. Apparently when three months were up they were ready to return, for that had been the time spent by their predecessors. However, they were informed, "Three months. Nobody said anything about three months." A short time later the *Jerusalem Post* carried the following item, June 14, 1970:

"Six prominent Gazans who were banished to Sinai by the Military Government in December last year, were allowed to return to their homes on Friday. . . .

"The six were dispersed among Beduin tribes in Sinai and have been under constant army supervision. They were allowed to return after they had pledged to refrain from all political and security activities in the future."

For persons such as these, whom Israel continues to arrest and detain, there should be some sort of Administrative Detention Camps, separate from common prisons and prisoners. For humanitarian reasons jails should be enlarged or new ones built.

Mr. Schlomo Hillel, head of Israel's police, is reported by insiders to be pressing for an improvement in the detention set-up and wants new prisons for political prisoners. There is some curious psychology here, though. Hillel is a Sephardim, from Iraq; he is one of the few Oriental or Arab Jews who has climbed to a rather important – if not the most enviable – post in the administration. His proposals have been flatly rejected by the European Israeli establishment, for whom "concentration camp" has connotations they want no part of in Israel.

So in Israel political prisoners, suspect because of their Arab race and Moslem or Christian religion, are picked up in the middle of the night and jammed into crowded cells or banished to the lonely desert.

Once in a while, among the grim tales in Occupied Territory, a story with an ironic twist is told. I was driving with a distinguished Arab woman to a frontier post with a special request for an elderly lady making a crossing. She had had to go first to the local military police to pick up instructions for the frontier; she was given an open note written in Hebrew. "I wish I could read this," she told me with some apprehension. "We must learn Hebrew. One of our people was given an unsealed note in Hebrew like this and took it to an Israeli official. It was instructions to arrest him and because he couldn't read Hebrew he didn't know."

Strangely, one of the problems contributing to the jail crowding is the difficulty young Palestinians are having getting into university. Before June 1967 most West Bank youngsters went to Amman, Beirut, or Cairo. The Palestinians have always had a great regard for higher education. Since June 1967, in order to go away to study, Israeli permission must be secured if they hope to return. Of course, young people can leave without a permit and with Israel's blessing but they won't get back. There are fifteen hundred Palestinians in Jordan University in Amman – half the undergraduate population – who can't return. A few study at Hebrew University, but most of them don't know Hebrew well enough; the courses available to them are limited, and some will not attend a Jewish university as a matter of principle. That makes for that many more unhappy and rebellious young people in Occupied Territory. Many have been arrested. After arrest they are held incommunicado for a period, and the family may hear its news through the prison grapevine.

Already a great Resistance folk-lore has been built up, and Palestine girls are developing a reputation for being harder to break than boys. One defiant girl from Ramallah refused to co-operate with her captors. Eventually the Israelis took her from Jerusalem to see her home blown up, apparently in an attempt to make her talk and serve as a lesson to her friends. As the house crumbled she made the traditional Arab trill of joy – and became an instant folk-heroine.

Along with this you hear of other stories of those who "sing" immediately and of prominent citizens who return broken and depressed to cease all protest. An observer cannot estimate the success of such Israeli policies. I know that immediately after 1967 the Israeli propaganda was that "there is no organized resistance;" then, when it began to show, the public policy was that it was ineffective and amateurish. Later, massive reprisals were instituted. Israel, despite the convictions of neutral observers, still seems to be convinced that if the Arabs are hit hard enough and often enough over the head they will knuckle under.

"It's a big psychiatric case," a psychiatrist who had worked in Palestine told me. "The Jews remember that the only way they were able to survive discrimination was to buckle under or pretend to. They think the Arabs will respond the same way. But the situation is different and the Arabs are a different kind of people."

One internationalist told me that the Israelis were betrayed by their inordinate concern for a single Jewish life and a tremendous preoccupation with personal security. "Have you noticed that they will exchange fifty Arabs to get back one captured Israeli? The whole nation is concerned about 'our boy.' When a commando is known to be hiding in a camp or has been hidden by someone, instead of risking a Jewish life to go and capture him the Israelis will blow up a house or two to teach a lesson. They don't get the commando but they make one hundred more."

twenty-five

Is There Anything We Can Do?

AS I WRITE THIS CONCLUDING CHAPTER, FOUR HUNDRED AND ninety-six thousand refugees huddle together against another winter in the wretched camps of Jordan and Syria. Tens of thousands are in tents with nothing but their hate to keep them warm. About seven hundred thousand Egyptians are crowded into temporary accomodation scattered all over the UAR, their former homes in rubble in the cities of the West Bank of the Suez Canal.

"Things get worse, and worse, and worse," Laurence Michelmore told me in his UNRWA office in Beirut in May. By November they were a lot worse. He was pleading with the UN in New York for six million dollars to provide the basic budget of forty-six million needed to provide subsistence, minimal health, and education for that portion of the one million four hundred thousand Palestinians on his rolls. If he didn't get it, the education of the young people would have to be cut away back. Education was their one hope to escape their degrading life. There were three hundred and forty-two thousand children among the refugees.

Russia was giving nothing to UNRWA, but provided arms to the Arab states. Canada gave no arms but sold parts and supplies to the Americans to give to Israel. Canada agreed to repeat the 1970 contribution of one million three hundred and fifty thousand dollars to UNRWA. The US continued to contribute about twenty-three million dollars to help the refugees.

While Michelmore begged for more help for the homeless, President Nixon gave another five hundred million dollars worth of arms to the Israelis. Mrs. Golda Meir boasted in Israel that it was "above anything" her country "ever dreamed of." General Dayan admitted they were as strong as they had been in 1967. That means a great deal stronger.

America's UN ambassador, Charles Yost, admitted to a group of church editors earlier in the year that "The Middle East is unquestionably the most threatening military situation in the world today." By December it had become even more threatening. It was tempting to give up hope.

The Arab world was apprehensive about the vacuum left by Nasser's death. In Northern Jordan the beaten fedayeen mourned the thousands who died in that late summer war between brothers. They nursed their wounded, attended their lectures, cleaned their weapons, and waited for another day. In Amman King Hussein's throne tottered.

The fedayeen could say, "At least the world noticed," as they remembered how they had hi-jacked three planes and eventually had blown them up, and had almost taken a fourth, and had held fifty-four passengers and crew hostage on the desert in exchange for six guerillas in Switzerland and Germany and a commando girl in London. The world had noticed, but did not like or understand that kind of war.

The Israelis diverted attention from central issues with repeated complaints that Egypt had violated an August 7th truce to end, temporarily, the fighting on the Suez. The West seemed to think it was unforgiveable for the Egyptians to arm their anti-aircraft defenses with missiles from Russia. Few pointed out that the missiles were to shoot down Israeli bombers on missions against Egyptian military and civilian targets. One would have thought by all the fuss that they were offensive weapons aimed at synagogues and hospitals in Tel Aviv and Jerusalem. In the meantime reports were published that during the truce that America was smuggling more Phantom bombers via Cyprus to Israel.

In the face of all this people continued to ask, "Is there anything the ordinary, decent, peace-loving person can do?"

163

For twenty-two years concerned people had asked such questions. Every time I write or speak about these things someone asks, "What can we do?"

The question is never asked, "Should we do anything?" We have a bad conscience over the Middle East. It was the anti-Semitism of the Christian world that made it necessary for the Jews to find a home of their own. It was our anti-Arabism that permitted us to provide a home at the expense of an innocent people. It was a combination of bad conscience and humanitarianism that made it necessary to assume responsibility for the new crop of persecuted people made homeless by our Balfour declarations and partition plans.

But even if we are not guilty, self-interest impels us to try to do something. There are many signs that America's next Vietnam will be in the Holy Land. It could bring about that threatened confrontation between the super-powers and involve us all.

Discouraging, almost hopeless though it seems to be, we can do something. There are three specific things I believe we ought to try to do.

We must press for a just settlement; we must contribute more generously to the support of the refugees and other displaced persons; we must inform ourselves on the complex Arab-Israeli problem. If we are to press intelligently for a settlement and give effective assistance to the homeless, we had better come to understand the issues. The communication of information and the development of understanding come first.

This is what the World Council of Churches and other concerned groups, which have made a study of the situation, have begun to say. At the end of a consultation on the Middle East, in Cyprus in late 1969, the WCC issued a statement which said: "We consider it an imperative obligation for all Christian Churches to . . . bring out responsibly, the facts about the Palestinian refugees and other displaced persons and the grave injustices done to the Palestinian people, so as to help create the conditions conducive to a just solution."

It has finally become obvious to enlightened churchmen that we have long been misled by false information, betrayed by our own mass media, including much of the religious press, and made victims of clever propaganda. Clergymen, especially, have been manipulated and intimidated by zealous Zionists. While the wcc and other informed groups of churchmen have been issuing such statements as that from Cyprus, other churchmen encouraged by free trips to Israel have become even more fanatic in their support for Zionism.

Dr. Roy Eckhardt, an American Methodist minister and Professor of Religion, told a clergy gathering in Houston, Texas, in January 1970, that "The proper place to give Christian witness today is in an Israeli munitions factory." The National Catholic Reporter rebuked Eckhardt sharply:

". . . . Israel is a modern civilized nation, and therefore its munitions factories make napalm. . . . Roasted Arab flesh is no more pleasing to God than the Vietnamese variety."

There is a deep gulf of divided opinion between Christians on this subject. Generally those who see the American war in Vietnam as a crusade for Christ and His Kingdom, who look under their beds for communists every night before they say their prayers, take the Eckhardt viewpoint. There are also liberals (who may bitterly oppose Vietnam) who have a sensitive understanding of anti-Semitism and know its fruits and who feel that to be pro-Jewish means they should support almost uncritically the policies of Israel and the philosophy of Zionism. "Anti-Zionism is the new anti-Semitism," they say.

At least those who travel to the Middle East *to both sides* and take a little time to study some of the objective reports and un documents know there are two or more sides. But such reports are sometimes difficult to get. In 1969 I published a list of books about the Middle East in the *United Church Observer*. It included such important titles as Davis's *The Evasive Peace* and Maxime Rodinson's *Israel and the Arabs* (a Penguin special). Readers who had taken the list in hand to their local libraries complained none of them was in stock. I did some checking and found the libraries I frequent had sections on the Middle East limited to pious little travelogues on the Holy Land.

If we are going to pay taxes to provide funds for the Middle

East, either weapons for Israel or food for refugees, we should be able to find out what we are paying for. We could study these matters in community and church groups. Our libraries should carry some of the excellent materials now available.

We should expect, too, that Holy Land "study tours" should go to both sides, and that editors and lecturers visit both sides before they write for and lecture to us. In 1969 the Associated Church Press and Catholic Church Press Associations in the US and Canada promoted a Middle East "study tour" for editors, which promised study on both the Arab and Israeli sides. It turned out that the subsidized tour was being assisted by an organization dedicated to Zionism. One editor who had written critical things about Israel had his money refunded and was dropped from the tour. But several dozen others took the junket and for months published their pieces about the wonders of Israel in the Christian press. That sort of thing has been going on for years in both religious and secular press. The most shocking distortions I have seen outside the religious press appeared in 1970 in the respected *Saturday Review of Literature*.

The Christian press and pulpit needs to take even more seriously than others the World Council of Churches appeal, for another reason. Not only have many editors and preachers sold their credibility for free trips to the Holy Land, they have distorted the Scriptures and misled their people. The WCC statement added an injunction: "The subject of Biblical interpretation (must) be studied in order to avoid the misuse (of the Bible) in support of partisan political views. . . ." In May 1970 a Beirut Conference of World Christians on Palestine put it more bluntly: "We reject the manipulation of Biblical texts for the purposes of political power."

A devout Catholic woman told me in Jerusalem, after listening to an articulate expression of the Palestinian view by an able professor, "I don't care what he says. The Bible says God gave Palestine to the Jews and that's enough for me." Strange though it may seem, such ideas apparently influenced such persons as Lord Balfour and General Allenby.

General E.L.M. Burns, Chief of Staff of the United Nations Truce Supervision Organization in Jerusalem from 1954-56, summarized:

166

"The United States Jewish community, through its economic power, especially as related to many media of mass information under the leadership of the well-organized Zionist pressure groups, exerts an influence on U.S. policy which goes far beyond what might be calculated from a counting of the so called Jewish vote.

"Over many years it is only Israel's side of the Palestine story which has been presented to Americans. The audience was pre-disposed to be sympathetic to Israel because of the horror the Nazi genocide had inspired, coupled doubtless with guilt feelings of those who have had anti-Semitic impulses. The picture of Israel as a small nation gallantly struggling to rebuild existence in its ancient home, a home guaranteed to it by the prophecies of the Bible, was accepted by a majority of the non-Jewish Americans and Canadians, especially those Christians who believe fervently in Biblican inspiration. Thus the Jews of the United States determine the degree of political as well as financial support that Israel receives from the U.S.A."

It is one of the great factors in Christian support for Zionist claims that "the Return" of the Jewish people and the expulsion of the Palestinians is simply a fulfillment of the promises of God and the prophecies of the Bible.

The simplest expression of the famous promise to God's Chosen People is found in Genesis 15:18. "Unto thy seed have I given this land from the River of Egypt (Nile) . . . unto the River Euphrates." Arabs point out that at that time Abraham had one son only, named Ishmael. They claim descent from Ishmael and that the Israelis descended from Isaac. There are more scholarly and theologically sound arguments than this.

The most important thing decent people can do is to let the facts be known – Biblical and otherwise.

Only an informed West can intelligently assist the Palestine refugees. They are fed up with charity and our patronizing attitude to "the poor refugee." But relief, distasteful though it is to the recipient and to the sensitive dispensers of it, must continue. There should be far more emphasis on education, training, and development. UNRWA is the most effective agency, but UNRWA work is hampered by an inadequate budget and malicious criticisms.

The Israelis don't like UNRWA for they know UNRWA workers are pro-Palestinian. UNRWA personnel have to be officially neutral. But they, like the personnel of all other agencies, suffer from exposure to the Middle East facts. UNRWA's work among the refugees attracts world attention to the continued plight of the displaced persons. Michelmore, for example, has consistently urged the return of the refugees who fled in 1967 to their homes and camps in Occupied Territory. The UN has continued to pass strong resolutions demanding their return. Israel ignores them; but Israel resents the criticism. It is suspected Zionists are behind the serious attempts to discredit UNRWA.

One of the worst hatchet jobs was done by Ira Hirschmann in *Look Magazine*, September 17th, 1968. Hirschmann charged that "between 200,000 and 500,000 of the refugees were non-existent ghosts." UNRWA immediately issued a forthright and documented denial, but the damage was done. Hirschmann's sensational "revelations" continue to appear in Zionist literature but, of course, without the denial.

UNRWA is also criticized, understandably, by the young Palestine commandos who have been fed in its kitchens and educated in its tents. They complain that UNRWA debilitated them; they note that Western nations which vote for their return to their homes in Palestine, and contribute to their fifteen hundred calories a day, also provide arms for Israel to prevent such a return. One commando girl in Irbid told me how she felt about this. "I hate UNRWA," she said, and when I asked, she added "The churches aren't quite as bad, except two." The two objects of her anger were the Mennonites and Quakers, who do fine work. "They teach our young people not to fight," she explained.

When WCC Secretary Eugene Carson Blake officially turned over fifteen hundred and twenty-two pre-fabricated shelters to the tented refugees in the Souf camp of Northern Jordan in March 1969, he said: "I think I hear you say, 'We are grateful for these shelters, but what we really want is to return to our own homes in Palestine.' " The shivering refugees didn't wait for the translation into Arabic. Their applause nearly brought down the tents.

The World Council said at Cyprus: "All our work of compassion should be done in the context of the struggle for a just solution." Repeatedly I heard Palestinians say, "It's not charity, it is justice we want."

We have to understand why the refugees don't want concrete shelters or to have anything done for their welfare that smacks of permanence. It has to be understood why the teaching of birth control to over-burdened Palestinian refugee women has to be done with care. Many of them – especially the Arab men, it seems to me – are determined to produce many sons to fight the Israelis and win back their homes. Whether the settlement comes tomorrow or tarries another decade, the homeless people have to be helped to live in dignity, and their children need be educated and trained for a productive future. For that, charity and handouts are not enough. In their present mood young Palestinians would rather be given a second-hand gun than a second-hand suit.

But what is the just solution for which we should work? In Israel there are hawks who propose "peace through annexation." And that is generally the way Israel moves. The World Jewish Congress's Nahum Goldmann proposed that Israel be neutralized and made into something between Switzerland and the Vatican. Yigal Allon has "The Allon Plan." Part of his plan is to succeed Mrs. Golda Meir. The same is true of General Dayan. Uri Avnery proposed that Israel should be de-Zionized and decent to Arabs. Many young Israelis echo his challenge.

Outside Israel, the two main proposals are well-known. The Palestine Liberation Organization proposes simply that they be allowed to return to their homes, where Christians, Moslems, and Jews, Arabs and Israelis and others, could build a democratic secular state with each man having one vote. This would bring an end to the Jewish dream of a Jewish state to which Jews from anywhere in the world might immigrate and become instant citizens.

Many responsible Arabs, and the governments of the UAR,

Jordan, and Lebanon, support the November 22nd, 1967, resolution passed unanimously by the Security Council. The resolution emphasizes "The inadmissability of the acquisition of territory by war and the need to work for a just and lasting peace in which every State in the area could live in security." Such a settlement would be based on two principles: (i) The withdrawal of Israeli armed forces from the territories occupied during the recent conflict; (ii) Termination of all claims and states of belligerency and respect for and acknowledgment of the sovereignty, territorial integrity, and political independence of every State in the area, and the right to live in peace within secure and recognized boundaries, free from threats or acts of force.

The resolution affirmed "the necessity for (a) guaranteeing freedom of navigation through international waterways in the area, (b) for achieving a just settlement of the refugee problem, (c) for guaranteeing the territorial inviolability and political independence of every State in the area, through measures including the establishment of demilitarized zones."

Such a proposal has been rejected by the Palestinian organizations, by Syria and Iraq and other distant Arab states. Certainly it would be unjust to the Palestinians, for it would secure Israel within the territories she acquired by force in 1948, far exceeding the area proposed by the partition. On the other hand, those who are ready to compromise say, "Is any settlement possible that would not be unjust to some groups? What about the Jews who emigrated in good faith to Israel from Europe or Arab countries? What about the Jewish children born in Israel since 1948?" It is obvious that no completely just settlement is possible. Those who approve the compromise hope that the "just settlement of the refugee problem," would mean, as the UN has often said, that the Palestinians would either return to their old homes in what is now Israel or be compensated.

November 22nd is the policy of most members of the UN. I have consistently supported it in my editorials, and in this I reflect the policy of my church and most churches belonging to the World Council. For this, of course, we have been criticized, but not unfairly, by the Palestinians. Church leaders in the Middle East issued an appeal to the churches of the world on November 22nd, 1968, urging Christians to press for such a settlement.

The question of whether we press for such a settlement seems to have become almost academic. Israel apparently has no intention of implementing the provisions, for it would mean withdrawing from Jerusalem and the plains of Syria. Israel has the rich tourist business, valuable agricultural lands on the Golan, and oil in the Sinai. With half a billion dollars more in arms from the US, she should be able to hold on indefinitely. She is like a child with a hand in the cookie jar. She would like peace but she wants the cookies.

Since 1967 Israeli spokesmen have implied they would settle on the basis of November 22nd. But in turn she insisted on not withdrawing from Jerusalem or the Golan, and she insisted on "direct negotiations." Direct negotiations, which seem reasonable enough to the uninformed, are politically impossible for the Arabs. For one thing, the Palestinians have no government or official voice to negotiate directly. No agreement made with the UAR or King Hussein could be made to stick. Further, "direct negotiations" is contrary to the Arab tradition and culture. Too often in modern times they have been betrayed.

Article thirty-five of the UN charter lists eight ways by which an international dispute may be settled: negotiation, arbitration, adjudication, mediation, conciliation, enquiry, use of regional agencies, and the UN General Assembly or Security Council. The Arabs say they are willing to seek settlement by any of seven; direct negotiation is not possible. The Israelis of course know this.

So what sort of a settlement can we realistically press for with any hope of fulfillment? Perhaps it is not necessary for us to back any given plan. I have supported November 22nd because I am not wise enough to come up with anything better than Lord Caradon and the Security Council have devised. But if the Arabs and Israelis could, with the help of the UN or someone, work out a settlement acceptable to them, that should make us all happy. But that is improbable. If Israel will not accept November 22nd and will not withdraw from territory taken in 1967, the Arabs are determined to take it back by force. Israel is reputed to have nuclear weapons now, and it must be assumed she will use them if she feels it is necessary.

I see no hope whatsoever in the present Israeli regime. Many, more expert than I, share the same cynicism regarding Mrs. Meir and those around her. Most Zionists abroad seem even more hawkish than she. The latest propaganda is that Israel is the West's bulwark against communism. Arabs point out that the policy of supporting Israeli expansion is pushing the whole Arab world into the communist camp.

But there is some hope in young Israelis and young Arabs, many of whom share the same view, that the Palestinians have been wronged, and the great hope for the future is for Israel to acknowledge the wrong and move to correct it.

The Jewish dream of a Jewish state at the moment of its apparent fulfillment has become a nightmare. Contrary to the highest ethical concepts of Judaism, Israeli Jews now practise racial discrimination. If they insist on maintaining the kind of Jewish state they have been building, they will have to continue to practise racism and apartheid. Such policies and practices nurture the seeds of anti-Semitism in the Middle East and abroad, and make a just peace impossible. I have confidence that world Jewry will eventually rid itself of Zionist fanaticism and racism. But that time is not yet. Perhaps it is wise for outsiders not to insist on any specific plan of settlement. We *should* insist that the unanimous decisions of the UN be enforced and the Geneva Conventions be kept. And we must urge our governments to press the UN to give top priority to the search for a just peace in the Middle East.

According to Maxime Rodinson, Ben Gurion is supposed to have said to his cabinet on the eve of the 1956 attack on the Sinai: "The Americans will force us to leave. America need send no troops to achieve that result; she need only state that she will break off diplomatic relations, prohibit collections for the Jewish fund, and block Israeli loans." President Eisenhower forced Israel to withdraw from Gaza and the Sinai.

We know that the Western nations could persuade Israel to adopt a more flexible policy. There is no sign that the Western nations will, or that public opinion would support such action if some courageous government were to take it.

Responsible government action will only follow pressure from informed public opinion. That is why the top priority for concerned people is to get the truth about the Middle East out to the world.

Postscript

Twelve months have passed since that last page was written. It was a good year for Israel, frustrating for the divided Arab world, tragic for the Palestinians, embarrassing to the United Nations, humiliating for the fedayeen and disastrous for the people of Gaza. It ended with an increased threat to world peace.

President Nixon assessed the situation by saying, "Vietnam is our most anguishing problem. It is not our most dangerous. That grim distinction goes to the Middle East with its vastly greater potential for drawing Soviet policy and our own into a collision that could be uncontrollable." Before he ended his distinguished career at the UN, Mr. U Thant said, "If the present impasse in the search for a peaceful settlement persists, new fighting will break out sooner or later."

The year brought rebukes and setbacks for the Israelis at the UN, new expressions of anger from the Asian and African nations, and at times tension with the US. But the year ended joyfully for them. Fifteen hundred immigrants a week were arriving from Russia, fedayeen attacks had ceased, and on December 30th Washington announced that the US would resume its delivery of F4 Phantom jets to Israel. There was jubilation in Jerusalem, and on December 31st, for the first time in more than a year, Palestine refugees in the hills of Jordan looked up to see Israeli military planes swooping in triumph over Amman. In early 1972 three Canadian cabinet ministers made pilgrimages to Tel Aviv, and Ottawa announced its intention of extending up to one hundred million dollars of long-term credit to Israel. Thus, in one quiet decision, unnoted by Canadian press and pulpit, Canada "loaned" five times as much to Israel as she had given in more than twenty years to UNRWA. The Canadian Zionist press was jubilant. It would be election year in the US and Canada, and Israel could count on North American support in 1972.

In Cairo, in late December, the heads of Egypt, Syria, and Libya (whose countries had banded together on August 20th to form the Federation of Arab States) pledged themselves to liberate all Arab territories occupied by Israel during the June 1967 war. So ended Anwar Sadat's "Year of Decision" announced on July 23rd – interpreted by some as a threat to go to war in 1971 if a political settlement were not reached.

In the new year Sadat began demanding more military aid from Moscow to offset the new Israeli arms and money from the West, and university students in Cairo held mass protests demanding war with Israel.

The year 1971 had been ushered in during an UN-imposed Suez cease-fire accepted by Israel and the UAR, with an Israeli cabinet decision to go back to the Jarring peace-talks. Mr. Jarring presented Israel and Egypt with a questionnaire on February 8th. Sadat replied on February 15th that in return for withdrawal by Israel from the territories taken in June 1967, Egypt would recognize Israel. Eleven days later Israel said flatly that she "would not withdraw".

On March 7th Sadat refused any further extension of the cease-fire, and on March 25th the Jarring mission was "frozen". The US Secretary of State tried again for agreement on "the Rogers Plan". On May 27th Egypt signed a treaty of friendship with the USSR. Cairo continued to build up her military strength with Russian help, Israel continued to expand and develop her Occupied Territories.

New Israeli apartments rose in Arab Jerusalem. New blocks of flats were built and occupied by Jewish settlers in Hebron. Mrs. Golda Meir announced that Sharm-el-Sheik would be added to the territories not to be given up in a future settlement, along with the Golan, Jerusalem, and Gaza. A string of new tourist hotels was erected at Sharm-el-Sheik and six million tons of oil were pumped in around-the-clock activity at Israel's new wells in the Egyptian Sinai. Feverish exploration and drilling continued.

Fedayeen attacks against Israel were almost ended, except in Gaza. In August, Israel moved to crush resistance in the Strip. Wide roads were bulldozed through several of the camps and another 2,400 Arab homes demolished. A British paper reported that when the 14,800 newly homeless crowded in with refugee relatives their condition was "an insult to a dead sardine". The new repressions were bitterly denounced by some Israeli intellectuals and The Israel League for Human Rights at Tel Aviv. Israel provided some housing in the desert for those who would take it, and offered cheap one-way fares to South America for those who would leave. Israel expropriated 8,500 acres of Arab land in Gaza for six new Jewish settlements. General S. Gazet said the Israeli intention was to remove "tens of thousands of Gazan people."

On August 19th, General Dayan said: "Israel . . . should move immediately to establish permanent government in the territories occupied since the six-day war."

In the face of such obvious intent the UN General Assembly on December 13th voted 79-7 for Israel to commit herself to withdraw from the Occupied Territory. Six South American countries voted with Israel; the US, Canada and 34 other countries abstained. How such countries justify abstention on an elementary principle, enshrined in the charter of the UN, and specifically outlined in the unanimous decision of the Security Council of November 22nd, 1967, was not explained.

After four and a half years of occupation, many of the 600,000 West Bank Arabs seemed to be finding a way to get along. Increasing numbers work in Israel. Since the September 1970 civil war and defeat of the East Bank Palestinians by Hussein, they suspect and hate the Jordan king almost as much as Israel. Palestine guerrillas, on November 28th in Cairo, assassinated Jordan Prime Minister Wafti Tel, and deepened the gulf between brothers. Israel refused to permit the return of

175

East Bank refugees to their homes and camps in the Occupied Zone, but many thousands were allowed back for a visit.

Early winter came to the 501,853 refugees in the UNRWA camps already shivering from the political events of the year. There were 6,000 more than a year ago, for Israel continues to expel a few, and more babies are born than old people die. The Russian winds swept down across the Turkish highlands and dumped their early snows on the tents and crude shelters of the 118,371 still in the ten emergency camps set up for the twice-displaced after the '67 war.

In Europe and North America some who have been contributing to the church and volunteer agency funds have begun to suffer from "compassion fatigue". The fifty million dollar UNRWA budget is still inadequate to maintain subsistence, health, and education for the people in the camps. There have been Biafra, Pakistan, and all those pictures of the bloated bodies and pinched faces of hungry children, and, for the Palestinian problem there seems no end. "I don't know how we can continue without cutting services," Sir John Rennie, who succeeded Laurence Michelmore at UNRWA, told me. He added enthusiastically that he was astonished by the number of Palestinians who made their way through university and found good jobs in the Arab world and beyond. Algeria is now looking to the Palestinians for teachers.

He praised and emphasized the need for continuing support from the churches and agencies, not only for the material assistance they provided but for educating the Western world to the problem. At Christmas, Monsignor John Nolan of the Pontifical Mission moved again through the camps encouraging the Catholic workers who, along with Lutherans, Mennonites, Friends, and representatives of most Christian churches, continue to serve. He arranged for a group of Bethlehem children to visit Pope Paul in Rome and through that visit reminded the affluent world of the continuing need, and the continuing work of the Church.

Although there has been an uneasy cease-fire on the Suez, there has been no cease-fire on the propaganda lines. The excellent Quaker report, "Search for Peace", from which I have quoted, was denounced by American Zionists as anti-Semitic, and a long refutation was published. "Search for Peace" is not available in Israel, but the angry Zionists' reply is.

A damning indictment of Israeli policies was made in October 1971 in the formal reports of the UN "Special Committee to investigate Israeli practices affecting the human rights of the population in the Occupied Territory". Some of my findings in chapters 16, 23, and 24, which had been attacked by Canadian Zionists as "fabrications", are corroborated in the Special Committee report to the UN. Their 1971 investigations "confirmed the impression" that Israeli "policies and practices violating the human rights of the population of the occupied territories have continued and even become more manifest". It pointed out that deportation of persons from occupied territory continues and is contrary to Article 49 of the 4th Geneva Convention. The committee added: "Israel's policy of destroying houses is in violation of Article 33 and 53 . . . and violates the fundamental human rights of the protected persons." The committee is of the opinion that "interrogation procedures very frequently involve physical violence".

The report of many pages echoes what has already been reported by the World Health Organization, Amnesty International, the International Red Cross, and is known to thousands of international workers in the Middle East. There has been very little publicity given to these findings outside the Middle East, and the "anti-Semite" label is likely to be attached to a writer or speaker who reports them from such UN documents.

In Israel itself a few voices of protest continue to be raised. They sound to me like Alan Paton in South Africa, clear, prophetic, courageous and, above all, right. But while the Israelis who protest the expansionist activities and suppressive policies of the Israeli government are among the ablest people of Israel, put them all together and they apparently have little political influence.

The present impasse reduced to its simplest formula is this: The Arab states of Egypt, Jordan, and Lebanon are still eager for a peaceful settlement on the unanimous terms laid down by the UN. However, if Israel will not withdraw to the 1967 boundaries, they see no recourse but eventual war to retake what has been taken from them. At the present time and into the foreseeable future it is believed by all experts that they would be beaten again. But, in the absence of a settlement and in the face of Israeli recalcitrance, they will continue to prepare for war by building up with military aid from Russia. Israel would like security, but not by paying the price of giving up her rich spoils of 1967, or ceasing her campaign to swell her population with Jewish immigrants from abroad. So she continues to develop the Occupied Territories, repress the inhabitants, expel or drive out all she can, and demand more weapons from the US. There is no sign that Israel will change her policies unless she is pressured by the US to do so.